OIL PAINTING PRINCIPLES AND TECHNIQUES

LESSONS OF ENZO RUSSO

Peter S. Robinson, David M. Renton and Eline de Jonge

Graphic Illustrations Peter S. Robinson

Photography
Robert F. Flood Jr.
Janna Fournier
Tiago Oliveira (AT Productions)
Janette Hoekstra (JHH Fine Art)
Kathleen F. Renton

Copyright Commentary
Mary Ann Fergus, Attorney at Law Specializing in Art Law

Edited by Kathryn Renton
Graphic Artist Cait Reiss

Front cover photography by Janna Fournier
Back cover portrait of Enzo Russo by Peter S. Robinson

Copyright 2008 by Peter S. Robinson and David M. Renton

All Rights Reserved. No part of this book may be reproduced or transmitted in any form without the express written permission from the authors, with the exception of brief excerpts for the purpose of critical review, promotion, or advertisement.

Published in the USA in 2008 by Renton Companies, Inc.

Correspondence: DT10@optonline.com
Publisher Website: www.enzorussofineart.com
ISBN 1434813959
Library of Congress Control Number: 2008932045

"I am often asked by students 'How long will it take to paint well?' That is the wrong question. The right question is 'How many paintings must one do before you paint well?' The answer probably is in the hundreds, so keep at it and don't get discouraged."

"An artist is always in need of experimentation, of exploring new possibilities, of pushing further and further. When an artist stops experimenting he or she is finished as a creator and has nothing more to contribute."

"Art is a means of communication … a channel to express our ideas, beliefs and feelings."

"Be painterly! Show your brush strokes."

Enzo Russo

CONTENTS

Preface — 13

Introduction by Enzo Russo — 15

Chapter 1: **The Nature of Light** — 17

Chapter 2: **Tools** — 21
- Paint — 21
- Painting Mediums — 22
- Solvents — 23
- Palette — 23
- Supports — 24
- Brushes — 25
- Knives — 26
- Easels — 27
- Studio — 28

Chapter 3: **Drawing and Composition** — 29
- Drawing — 29
- Format and Composition:
  - Abstract Design — 30
  - Balance — 30
  - Tension — 30
  - Focal Point — 30
  - The Rule of Thirds — 30
- Positive and Negative Space — 31
- Edges — 32
- Light and Dark – The Value Scale — 33
- Form and Volume – The Illusion of Depth — 33
- Perspective – Linear and Aerial — 34
- Shadows — 35
- Five Dynamics of Light:
  - Light — 35
  - Highlights — 35
  - Proper Shadow — 35
  - Cast Shadows — 35
  - Reflected Light — 36

CONTENTS

Chapter 4: Color — 37

- Primary Colors — 37
- Secondary Colors — 37
- Tertiary Colors — 38
- Color Harmony — 38
- Properties of Colors:
  - Hue — 38
  - Value — 38
  - Temperature — 39
- Chroma — 39
- White and Black — 39
- Color and Shadows — 40
- Thick and Thin — 40
- Highlights and Glare — 41
- Dynamic Grays — 41
- Transparency — 41
- The Artist's Palette — 42

Chapter 5: Conceptual Principles — 47

- Being Painterly — 47
- Concept — 47
- Contrast and Variation — 47
- Motion — 49
- Painting from Photographs — 49
- Copyright Issues — 49
- Work the Whole Canvas — 49
- Unity of Style — 50

CONTENTS

Chapter 6: **Techniques** 51

    Standard Painting Techniques:

        Staining the Canvas   51

        Wet-on-Wet   51

        Glazing   51

        Scumbling   52

        Dry Brush   52

        Blending Edges   53

        Cross Hatching   53

        Impasto   53

        Pattern and Texture   53

        Rags and Rubbing   53

        Use a Large Canvas   54

    Techniques for Specific Genres:

        Landscape   55

        Marine Painting   58

        Still Life   61

        Portraits   63

Chapter 7: **The Painting Process** 73

    Plan Your Painting   73

    Block in the Painting   74

    Refine Your Painting   75

    Know When to Stop   76

CONTENTS

Chapter 8:	**After the Painting Is Finished**	77
	Signature	77
	Protecting Your Painting	78
	Framing	79
	Photographing Your Painting	79
Chapter 9:	**Marketing Your Work**	83
Chapter 10:	**Conclusion**	87
Appendix A:	**Enzo Russo Biographical Notes**	90
Appendix B:	**Copyright and Other Legal Considerations**	93

ILLUSTRATIONS

Diagrams

Prismatic Light	17
Reflected Light	18
Three Sources of Light	19
Pigments	21
Units of Measurement	29
Negative Space	31
Types of Edges	32
Value Scale	33
Linear Perspective	34
Five Dynamics of Light	35
Producing Complements	37
Color Wheel	37
Mixing Complements	38
Juxtaposing Complements	39
Double Primaries and Secondaries	44
Glazing	52
Scumbling	52
Photographing Your Painting	79

Photographs

Enzo Russo with students at MOMA	13
Traditional Palette	23
Canvas Stretching Tools	24
Filbert Brushes	26
Painting Knives	26
Easels	27
Rule of Thirds	31
Types of Edges	32
Foreshortening	36
Blue Family	42
Enzo Russo's Palette	43
Enzo and Germano Russo	90

Paintings of Eline de Jonge

Shadows and Light Grand Central II	48
Shadows and Light Grand Central III	48
Shadows and Light Grand Central	76

ILLUSTRATIONS

Paintings of Susan Kalla
Boy in Water	50
Block-in for Oil Painting on Canvas	74

Paintings of David M. Renton
Lumber Schooner George W. Collins	58
Working Tug D. M. Renton	59
No Wind	94

Paintings of Peter S. Robinson
Portrait of Enzo Russo	14
Block Island Lighthouse	77
Theresa	96

Paintings of Enzo Russo
Portrait of a Dutch Lady	20	Portrait of a Boy	68
Portrait of a Young Woman I	31	Portrait of an Equestrian	71
Child at the Beach	32	Balancing Act on Marshall Street	72
Portrait of a Violinist	36	Autumn	82
America	45	Ladies of the Night	86
Cabaret Series	46	Cabaret Singer	88
Shimmering Sails of Menton	54	Eiffel Tower Vision	89
Schooner Alberta	61	Portrait of a Young Boy	89
Portrait of Susan Kalla	63	Portrait of William Evart	89
Portrait of a Young Girl	64	Girl in Chair	92
Portrait of a Young Woman II	66	Portrait of Doug Birdsall	102

Paintings of Germano Russo
Tuscan Landscape Drawing	28
Pen and Ink Sketch	53
Tuscan Landscape Painting II	56
Tuscan Landscape Painting	57
Tuscan Landscape Painting III	57
Flowers and Vase	62

Painting of Karen Spring
Portrait of a Young Woman II	66

PREFACE AND DEDICATION

The purpose of this book is to set down lessons that Enzo Russo has taught his students regarding principles and techniques of oil painting. We trust we have done so in a practical, easily learned and readily implemented manner. The most interesting and important pieces of information – those that especially warrant the writing of this book – concern Enzo Russo's opinions and insights about art in general, painting in particular, and the advice he offers. These are many and often surprising.

Nearly all of Enzo Russo's long life has been spent doing the two things he loves most – painting and teaching others how to paint. He is an exceptional artist and an extraordinary teacher who has been generous with his time, enabling his students to learn and grow in their art. He passes on to them a wide range of knowledge that is based on his superb academic training in Florence, long professional experience, and understanding of classical and contemporary art (see Enzo Russo Biographical Notes page 90). More importantly, he inspires and challenges his students to develop a critical awareness that opens up new avenues for them to explore. He does all of this with great humor and affection for those he teaches, no matter their age or level of experience.

We dedicate this book to Enzo Russo, whose teaching and personality have deeply impacted our lives, and to his identical twin brother Germano, a fellow artist and Enzo Russo's closest friend.

Enzo Russo (left) leads a group of his students through the Museum of Modern Art in New York. The paintings in the background are by his revered teacher, Giorgio de Chirico, the father of Surrealism.

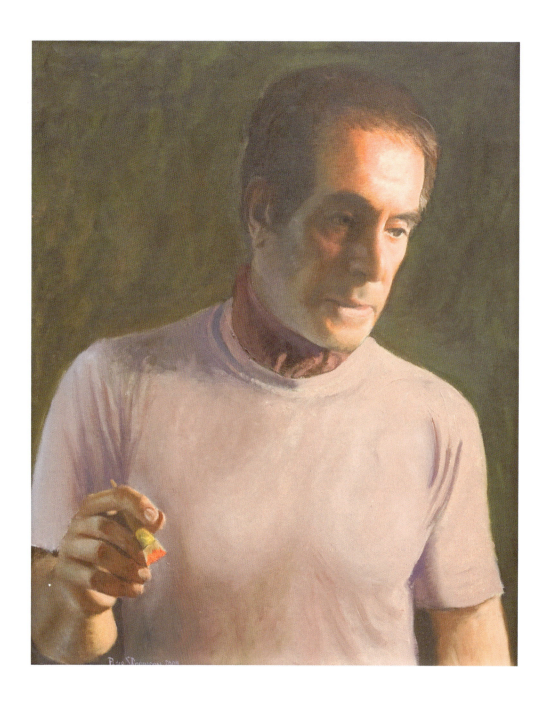

Peter S. Robinson
Portrait of Enzo Russo
oil on canvas, 24"x30"

INTRODUCTION
By Enzo Russo

Teaching is a natural gift born of an instinct to communicate and explain. When my twin brother Germano and I were about twelve, our mother joked about our distinctive characters and had a nickname for each of us. She fondly referred to Germano, who would never stop talking, as "the lawyer," and she called me "the teacher." That, she joked, was what I was going to be when I grew up. She didn't know how right she was.

Over a lifetime as an artist and a teacher I have never stopped reflecting on the rewards, the frustrations, the abilities and feasibilities of being a teacher. As I am now in the last chapter of my life, it has become increasingly clear that teaching art is an art in itself, quite different from teaching other disciplines. To begin with, it is crucial to realize that in all of the arts there are no absolutes, no incontrovertible truths, no axiomatic fixed points. Unlike in science and mathematics, the "numbers" in the arts are never fixed entities. They are mutating all the time due to our exclusively subjective observations of objective reality.

Hence, any creative act is a blend of objective reality and creative reality, to which the rules and logic of the physical world therefore do not inevitably apply. Subjective interpretation and the uniquely human ability to imagine and to foresee are characteristics of the artist. That is precisely why, in making a work of the imagination, creative goals justify the conceptual manipulation of the objective world. That is also the point where the teaching of art and the teaching of objective disciplines tend to separate, before they finally come together again at the end of the full circle.

From the time we were cave dwellers, we have been driven by the mysterious impulse to draw what we see. Although it took us a very long time to discover the hidden laws which govern the phenomenon of vision, those revelations enabled us eventually to formulate the principles, define the rules and develop the methods by which we could quite convincingly create the illusion of three-dimensional reality on a two-dimensional surface. The principles of perspective were foremost among these discoveries.

This quest for unlocking the secrets of visual reality took place over many centuries and occupied nine-tenths of the entire history of art. Only toward the end of the nineteenth century, when a generation of young and middle-aged artists were preparing to experience the promises and uncertainties of a new era, did a second wave of discovery occur that rivaled that of perspective. This second most important art revolution took everyone by surprise and just as swiftly began to unlock the remaining secrets of visual reality. The age of photography was born and our visual perception of life and the world has never been the same since.

The invention of photography was indeed a significant moment in the history of the visual arts and yet, by the same token, it was to become a kind of perverse paradox. By enabling us to unlock the final secrets of the visual puzzle, we began to discover that our now near perfect ability to reproduce accurately all that we see failed to convey our emotions. For all of its exactitude, the new invention of photography could not reveal to the viewer the artist's most intimate and personal message, the one coming from the heart.

It did not take as long as conquering the visual reality for a group of bold young artists to realize that in order to convey one's subjective responses to life and to the world, one must "disturb" the accuracy and the objectivity of what one looks at and chooses to represent. In short, we must go beyond the measurable reality of the subject, go beyond realism. It is in this realization that modern art was born and set on its controversial yet courageous journey to new creative frontiers.

I see many hopeful signs for the future of visual arts. America and the other parts of the industrialized world are discovering art as one of the surest, maintenance-free, and steadily appreciating investments. Huge corporations in western countries, as well as Japan and now China, are purchasing art both as an investment and mark of prestige for their headquarters. Consequently many young people today are looking at art as a lucrative career, not only as a field to express their creativity. The visual arts are being rekindled by a new kind of humanism that seems to bring the arts back to their responsibility towards life. It is a good time to be an artist today.

Through the years, I have been involved in all the various art techniques: oil, water color, tempura, acrylics, pastels, frescos and others. But my personal preference is for oil. Oil painting is the most benign medium in the visual arts, aesthetically speaking. No other medium is as obedient, cooperative, and fascinating, but unfortunately also so fragile. For this reason I have become a serious student of oil's chemical properties and of the lethal assault of time on its uniquely beautiful surface. As a consequence, I make an effort to alert and inform my students about how to avoid oil's shortcomings.

I hope my students will take away from my teaching a rock solid technique based on time-honored principles. My goal is for them to become acutely aware that in making a work of the imagination, technical matters and the painting concept invariably are of greater importance than lofty pronouncements and philosophical acrobatics. But most of all I want my students to have faith in their own work and in their mission as creative individuals. I want them to recognize relevance in the most humble of things. I want them to realize that a truly creative effort is always important because it is a record of a thinking entity blessed with the gift of imagination. Ultimately, I hope they will realize that civilizations are never measured by the bottom line, but rather by the arts and the ideas they produce and pass on to later generations.

CHAPTER 1

THE NATURE OF LIGHT

Enzo Russo emphasizes that light is elemental to painting. All we see around us is light that is reflected off various objects, impressed on the optic nerves in our eyes, and then passed along as electric impulses to and interpreted by our brains. This is known as the "visual system." This process of "seeing" and all the nuances involved therein are important to understand as they directly affect how we paint, what we see and what we choose to paint. This chapter will provide that background.

Sunlight is the visible segment of the spectrum of electromagnetic radiation produced by the nuclear combustion of the sun. The spectrum is a continuum of energy waves, including ones that are familiar to us, such as radio waves, x-rays, microwaves and of course light.[1] The wavelengths at one end of the spectrum measure more than thousands of miles across. The wavelengths at the other end measure less than the width of an atom.

PRISMATIC LIGHT

Within the range of visible light, the varying size of the wavelengths determines the colors we see. From short to long, these are Violet, Blue, Green, Yellow, Orange, and Red. The combination of all of the visible waves results in "white" light or sunlight. A prism is able to split white light so we can see its component colors. A moist atmosphere can function as a prism, producing a rainbow. The splitting process is known as refraction. The upper atmosphere refracts sun light in a manner such that we only see the color blue in the sky.

Visible light comes from natural and articficial sources. Sunlight, skylight and candlelight are examples of natural light. Artificial light comes from an electric source. Examples are incandescent filament bulbs and fluorescent tubes. Of all of these forms of emitted light, only sunlight contains the full spectrum of color. The warm colors predominate in light produced by candles and filament bulbs, whereas the opposite is true in the case of florescent light.[2] Skylight, of course, is predominantly blue (cool) for the reason mentioned above.

At dawn and dusk, sunlight passes through a thicker layer of atmosphere than at noon, when the sun is directly overhead. The thicker atmosphere effectively filters out the cooler colors of the light spectrum, resulting in a warm (red-orange) cast to the light that reaches

---

1 Sorted by wave length, short to long, the electromagnetic spectrum consists of: gamma rays, x-rays, ultraviolet visible spectrum, infared, terahertz radiation, microwaves and radio waves.
2 Consequently don't photograph your paintings in early morning light. It is too warm. Wait until at least 10 AM in summer time, and at noon in winter. Winter light compared to summer light is optically warmer because the sun is lower on the horizon.
3 The space above the atmosphere – cosmic space – is black, speckled with pin points of star light. It is black because there is no air, dust or moisture to refract or reflect the sun's light.

us. Noon light is relatively cooler because the spectral color balance is restored due to the thinner atmosphere.[3] The daytime blue color of sky light illuminates shadows, causing them to appear slightly blue or purple.[4] This is particularly evident in snow. In the northern hemisphere, many artists' studios have the skylight oriented to the north because the sun never appears in the northern sky, leaving it as a source of steady, even and cool light during the day. Moonlight, which is reflected sunlight, is also cool, and the night landscape it illuminates takes on a bluish cast.

Our Reaction to Light

The nature of light is not just physical. It is also physiological and psychological. Each of us experiences light differently depending on our physiological make up. An extreme case is color blindness in which an individual is incapable of seeing certain colors. We learn to associate colors with sensations. For example, we associate red and yellow with warmth and fire, while we associate blue and purple with cold and ice. We also associate colors with emotions. Taking advantage of this natural reaction to color, the Philadelphia Police Department decided to change the color of its patrol cars from red to blue– red generates feelings of anger and passion, and blue feelings of calm and peacefulness. By his choice of color the artist can affect the viewer's psychological response to his painting.

Reflected Light

Painting is conditioned not only by emitted light, but also by *reflected* light. Indeed, physically what the viewer sees when looking at a painting is the light it reflects.[5] The reflection is selective in as much as what is reflected consists of colors in the emitted light that are not absorbed by the painting. For instance, a spot of red paint absorbs all other prismatic colors except red, which it reflects. A white surface absorbs the least amount of light because it reflects all colors, whereas a matted black surface does the opposite, absorbing all of the colors and, therefore, the maximum amount of light.[6]

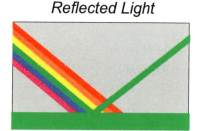

Reflected Light

The green surface absorbs all colors except green, which it reflects.

---

4 There are some lamps on the market that attempt to approximate the spectrum balance of sun light. Many artists use these to illuminate their easels and studios.
5 Paint cannot emit light, yet landscape painters have to simulate natural, emitted light with reflected light when painting the sun and sky. They do this by contrasting light against dark and by achieving the effect of luminosity through glazing (discussed later).
6 This is why you should use a black cloth without a sheen as a backdrop when photographing your paintings.

CHAPTER 1 – NATURE OF LIGHT

The particular color components of the light illuminating a painting will significantly affect its appearance. Only those colors in the painting that correspond to colors in the illuminating light will be reflected and reach your eye. The other colors in the painting will appear dull and dark. Recall your experience in a photographer's darkroom lit only by a red light in which everything appears red. Although the color of reflected light is conditioned by the color of the original light source, it is also affected by the color of the object from which it is reflected. For instance, white light reflected from a red tablecloth will cast a red tint on objects resting on it, such as plates and saucers. The painter must show this happening *within* the painting.

Whether or not he or she is aware of it, the painter always deals with three sources of emitted light: that which illuminates the subject matter, that which illuminates the palette and canvas, and that which illuminates the finished painting. One needs to be aware of the predominant color temperature of the light sources because they condition the color and temperature of the painting. The ultimate factor conditioning the appearance of a painting is the light that illuminates it when it is finished and hanging on someone's wall. Florescent lighting in the room will heighten the cool colors in the painting, whereas a filament light will heighten the warm colors. An artist should advise the purchaser of the painting about which kind of light would be appropriate for the painting. Be aware that the wrong lighting can diminish the painting.

Three Sources of Light

The color temperature of the light illuminating the scene or subject of a painting can vary significantly from that lighting the canvas and palette if in shadow. So be aware of the difference to make the necessary allowance. The light illuminating the finished painting will also affect its colors, but that is usually beyond the control of the artist.

Enzo Russo
Portrait of a Dutch Lady
Mrs. Elizabeth Spor
oil on canvas 30" x 30"

CHAPTER 2

TOOLS

Like all professionals, artists rely on a basic set of tools to practice their craft. The most indispensable of these is the paint itself.

Paint: Paint consists of color pigments suspended in a medium. The medium will vary depending on the type of paint. Oil paints usually contain linseed oil. Acrylic and watercolor paints contain water. As the medium dries, it leaves behind the color pigment bound to the "support" – i.e., canvas, board, etc. Oil paint dries differently than do acrylics and watercolor. The latter two dry when their water mediums evaporate, a process which is relatively fast. Oil, on the other hand, dries by oxidizing – taking on oxygen - which is a much slower process.

Whereas oil paint, depending on its thickness, can take as much as a week to dry to the touch, a far longer time is required for it to dry completely – months, if not years. However oil paint is usually dry enough after at least one month to apply a protective cover. As will be mentioned later, Enzo Russo strongly recommends protecting the painting by waxing it, and avoiding the use of a varnish. In contrast to oil paint, acrylic and watercolor dry thoroughly in a matter of minutes.

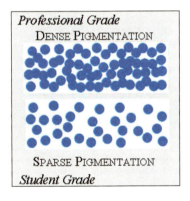

The market factor that determines the price of oil paint is the quality and quantity of pigments used in the paint. The so-called "student" grade paints have fewer and inferior pigments and more medium per volume measure than do the "professional" grade. This affects the painting process in a number of ways. Student grade paints are more "watery" whereas professional grade paints are dense with pigment.[7] The color saturation or intensity of student grade paints is therefore significantly less than professional grade paints. You will find that the price of a tube of paint also varies according to the color of the paint. This price difference is caused by the relative costs of the pigments used. The scarcer the pigment, the more expensive it is.

The history of pigments is a fascinating one. The original ultramarine, created from crushed lapis lazuli, was much more valuable than gold. Some purple pigments were only allowed to be used for the benefit of royalty with death as the punishment for transgression of the rules. Pigments are derived from earth, bugs, chemicals, cow's urine, precious stones, dyes, and other materials from all over the world.[8]

---

[7] Using paint that is too oily will cause the painting to deteriorate sooner than otherwise. You can blot up the excess linseed oil by first placing the paint from the tube onto a paper towel, which will absorb the excess oil, at which point you can use your palette knife to lift the remaining paint from the towel and place it on the palette.

[8] Read Victoria Finla's book Color (Random House, NY, 2004) for a fascinating account of what and how pigments were used by artists through the ages.

Oil or Acrylic: Which one should you use? Acrylic paints are synthetic and water solvent. Their advantage over oil paint is that acrylics are less expensive and less toxic (no turpentine or other hazardous solvents required). The latter is reason enough for some artists not to use oils.

Acrylics also dry very fast whereas oil paint dries very slowly. This is an advantage in that you do not have to wait very long before you can apply another coat of paint, as when glazing multiple layers of paint. On the other hand, it is a disadvantage because it makes mixing and blending paints more difficult than with slow drying oils, especially on the canvas. Individual oil paints have varying drying times. For instance, raw sienna and cobalt blue dry in two days or less whereas it can take four or five days for alizarin crimson or titanium white to dry to the touch.

For Enzo Russo, oil paints are far superior to acrylics for the following reasons. Oils blend more easily and attain a smooth transition from dark to light or from warm to cold. They are more capable of transparency than acrylics. Unlike acrylics, oil dries without a substantial change in value and chroma. The intensities of oil colors will remain the same when the paint dries, but this is not the case with acrylics. Oil conveys a sense of richness in the overall appearance of the painting which is reinforced by a particular luster which acrylics cannot achieve. These are no doubt among several of the reasons why oil paintings are priced higher on the market than acrylic paintings.

Although this book is primarily about oil painting, most of what is said also applies to acrylic and other mediums.

> **Mediums can...**
>
> - Thin or thicken paint
> - Give it a glossy or matte appearance
> - Hasten or delay drying

Painting mediums: A variety of mediums are available to thin or thicken paint or to cause it to dry slowly, rapidly, or to dry with a sheen or matte finish. In oil painting, the most commonly used thinning medium is linseed oil, combined in some measure with turpentine or mineral spirits[9] and sometimes also with damar varnish. There are other medium options for oil paint, the most important of which is wax. Enzo Russo strongly advises his students to use wax[10] and eschew turpentine and mineral spirits, which are solvents. He explains that all solvents, turpentine and mineral spirits included, cause the molecules of the linseed oil in the paint to separate when completely dried, rendering it liable to chipping, cracking or flaking in the long run.

---

9 Turpenoid and Sunnyside Oderless Paint Thinner are two popular brands of mineral spirits.
10 The brand Enzo and many of his students use is Dorland's Wax Medium.

CHAPTER 2 – TOOLS

By contrast, he explains, wax prevents the paint surface from cracking no matter how thick the paint. In addition wax causes the paint to dry harder and faster. Wax also serves to make the paint "buttery," which facilitates impasto painting – paint applied very thickly. Mixing wax with paint also extends the amount of paint you have to work with. Any fear one may have of the wax in the painting melting is misplaced. This will not happen unless the painting is held in very close proximity to a flame or extremely hot object.

Used alone as a medium, linseed oil can also cause the paint surface to crack over time. The risk of cracking increases when linseed oil is mixed with student grade paints, which already have a high proportion of the oil.

For acrylics and watercolor, water is the primary medium used to dilute the paint. Although the medium of acrylic paints is water, there are other ingredients one can add to make it dry more slowly, to thicken it, or to make it dry "flat" or "glossy."

Solvents: Turpentine, mineral oil and other kinds of solvents are used to clean one's brushes of oil paint and to clean up spilled paint.

Palette: The palette is the surface on which you place and mix your paints for application on your canvas. Palettes come in different materials, sizes and shapes. The traditional palette for oil painting is made of a hard wood with a thumb hole. This type of palette is convenient for painting outdoors (in *plein air*). A simple piece of glass placed over white or neutral color paper or cardboard makes an excellent studio palette. This is what Enzo Russo uses and recommends. It is easy to work with and to clean, and its non-absorbent surface slows down the drying process.

Some people prefer a paper palette that can be discarded after the painting session is over, making the clean-up easier. Enzo Russo does not favor this because it usually results in an unjustifiable waste of paint, which after all is not cheap. Rather than throw the unused

Traditional Palette

paint away, scrape it up and place it in two piles, one for warm colors and one for cool, on the periphery of your palette for use later. Then, thoroughly clean the mixing area of the palette and submerge the palette in water. Better still, put it in the freezer for later use. The paint will remain supple for a long time.[11]

Supports: "Support" is the word given to the object on which one does the painting. Typically, the support is a cotton or linen fabric stretched over a wood "stretcher" (making a "canvas") for oil and acrylic painting. But the support could also be paper, wood, composite board such as masonite, glass, stone and other kinds of surfaces. For watercolor the support is almost always paper.

Canvas Stretching Tools

Which is better for oil painting, cotton or linen? Linen fabric usually keeps taught longer than cotton. However, when your canvas appears slack you can very easily remedy the problem by following these steps. Put the painting upside down on a table. Using a bowl of hot water and a clean sponge, thoroughly dampen the rear side of the canvas. Be careful not to wet the wooden stretcher as it may warp. Put the canvas back on its side and let it dry in a warm room or outside in the sun.[12] Very soon the canvas will become taut. You can also tighten the canvas by tapping wood or plastic wedges into the inside corners of the stretcher, which expands the perimeter of the stretcher.

Linen is more expensive than cotton fabric. With both linen and cotton, the thickness and weight of the fabric vary. The thickness and weight should increase in proportion to the size of the canvas desired. A great advantage of cotton over linen, besides price, is that it will not deteriorate.

Should you stretch your own canvases or buy them ready made? It is certainly more convenient to buy readymade canvases and there is not much cost difference in the case of small canvases. However, in the case of large canvases (more than 30 x 40 inches), stretching your own is cheaper and generally better in that you can choose the weight of the fabric and the size (strength) of the wood frame. The sturdier the wood, the less chance the frame will warp. Enzo always stretches his own canvases because that way he controls everything in the process – the quality of the fabric and stretcher and the proper application of the primer.

---

11 For acrylic paints you should use a shallow plastic box with a wet sponge at the bottom covered by a tough paper on which to place and mix the paints. (Masterson makes such a device).The moisture in the sponge seeps through the paper and keeps the acrylic paint from drying. When the painting session is over one applies a hard cover that makes the plastic box airtight, keeping the paints wet. If you don't use this type of tray you will find it essential to have an atomizer at hand filled with water to spray the acrylic paints on the palette to keep them from dying out.

12 Let the canvas stand on one side for five minutes and then turn it over on the other side.

CHAPTER 2 – TOOLS

An electric staple gun will ease the process of stapling the canvas to the stretcher.[13] Canvas pliers are required to pull the canvas taut, always beginning in the middle of each side and then, in a balancing fashion, on opposing sides, alternately stapling the canvas in one inch increments towards the corners.

Once you stretch the fabric you have to prepare it to receive paint.[14] There are several substances you can use, but the easiest is an acrylic gesso that you brush on. This material, which comes in varying colors, is inexpensive and readily available in any art supply shop. By applying at least two coats and sanding with sandpaper between coats you can achieve as rough or smooth a surface as you desire. A two or three-inch house painting brush is ideal for priming.

Brushes: The most versatile instrument for applying paint to the support is the brush. Although you can paint with a palette knife or other more exotic devices, the most common way is to use brushes. In addition to the sheer facility of brushing paint on the support, the imprint of the brush strokes is crucial to the self expression of the artist. Indeed, the brushwork should be regarded as a kind of signature of the artist. It is certainly a vital factor to the "painterly" quality of the painting and should be evidently so. For these reasons Enzo Russo notes that the quality and durability of the brushes ought to be of prime consideration to the artist, even more so than the quality of the paints. Consider this: you end up spending more money buying cheap brushes than buying quality ones because the cheap ones wear out much more quickly.

Brushes come in varying materials, sizes and shapes. For oil and acrylic painting, the brushes are made with strong elastic bristles.[15] Watercolor brushes are made with soft, pliant fibers, such as sable hair or its synthetic equivalents. Brushes are numbered by size; the smaller the number the smaller the size. At a minimum the artist should have #2, #4, #6, and #8 brushes, plus one or more very small brushes for detailed work. Because of the importance of visible brushwork the artist should consider using the largest brush appropriate to achieve the effect desired.

Brushes come in standard shapes. "Flats" have bristles that end in a flat, linear edge. Turned sideways, flats are good for painting short lines and sharp edges. "Rounds," as the name implies, have bristles that are rounded and pointed at the tip. Rounds are good for painting long lines, especially one particular variety of rounds, the so called "rigger." Rigger brushes have very long bristles (capable of holding a lot of paint) and can be used to paint fine detail, such as a ship's rigging.

---

13 Power Shot Pro heavy duty electric staple and nail gun
14 In former times a glue made from rabbit skin was used for this purpose, effectively sealing the spaces between the fabric's fibers preventing the absorption of the oil medium in the fibers. This process was known as "sizing."
15 The common natural bristle for oil paint brushes is hogs hair. But there are several synthetic fibers that are less expensive, easy to clean and just as effective.

"Filberts" are like flats except the bristles are tapered at the tip. Filbert brushes have the most versatility, so much so that Enzo Russo advises that they should be used most often, even exclusively. Make sure the brushes have relatively long bristles, capable of holding a lot of paint while remaining resilient.

The rough surface of the canvas gradually wears away a brush's bristles. Discard the brush before the bristles become mere stumps. The brushes are no good at that point, except for scratching and scumbling, because they cannot hold paint and have lost their elasticity. When applying paint to the canvas, avoid pushing the brush with the bristle forward as this is harmful to the bristles and causes them to lose shape.

Thoroughly clean the brushes of paint immediately after a painting session. Do this by wiping on a towel (paper or cloth) any excess paint on the brush, steeping the brush in turpentine or mineral spirits to dissolve the remaining paint, and then wiping the bristles with a clean paper towel or cloth rag. Do this until all traces of the paint are removed from the bristles. When dipping the brush in the solvent be sure the bristles do not rub against the sides or bottom of the solvent container. Doing so clouds the solvent with paint.

You can clean multiple brushes of the same size at the same time. Just hold four or five brushes in your hand and go through the cleaning process. This shortens the time it takes to put things away. Enzo advises you not wash the bristles in soapy water after cleaning them with a solvent. Water, he explains, is harmful to the oil residue in the bristles. Brushes used for acrylic painting, on the other hand, must be cleaned with water because acrylics are only water soluble.

While you are painting, wipe clean your brushes often with rags or paper towels. This keeps the paint clean. Do not skimp on paper towels or cloth rags. You can also keep paint dollops on your palette clean by using a knife rather than a tainted brush to cut out paint for mixing. Use multiple brushes for different colors.

Knives: Two kinds of "knives" are used in oil and acrylic painting. The "palette" knife has a flat blade and is used for mixing paint on the palette and scraping the whole or portion of the palette clean. The "painting" knife resembles a trowel and is used to apply paint on the support. In fact, the painting knife is all that is needed because it can serve all three functions. It is convenient to have a small one to mix or apply small amounts of paint and a large one to do the same for large

Painting knives

CHAPTER 2 – TOOLS

amounts of paint, plus to clean the palette. Use a clean knife, rather than your brushes, to dip into the paint so the paint pile stays clean.

Easels: There are a wide variety of easels to choose among. Your choice should be based on the following factors in addition to price: the space available in your studio, the size of paintings you will be doing, and whether you will be painting indoors or in plein air.

A simple and fairly inexpensive easel is an A-frame tripod model that can be folded and set aside. For outdoor painting a French box easel or pochade box easel is recommended because it has storage space for your paints and mediums and can be neatly folded up for carrying.

Enzo Russo's advice when choosing a studio easel is to give primary consideration to its weight. The heavier the easel, the sturdier and more stable it is. Sturdiness is particularly important when painting large canvases. Enzo Russo says it is better to buy a large easel initially because as you gain experience you will graduate to larger and larger canvases.

Studio easel

Plein air pochade box easel.

French box easel

Studio: If possible, dedicate a room in your house to your painting. That way you will not have to set up and take down your equipment for every painting session, and you can furnish the room with the cabinets, counter tops and shelving to store your implements and paints. Paint the walls white for maximum reflection of natural light. The more natural light available in the room the better. The quality of light illuminating your easel should be the same for your palette. With oil paints and solvents, it is important that the studio room is adequately ventilated.

Germano Russo
Tuscan Landscape
charcoal drawing on paper

CHAPTER 3

DRAWING AND COMPOSITION

Drawing

The essential role of drawing in painting is to indicate the shape and placement of the objects in the painting. Drawing on the support can be done with charcoal or with a brush using diluted paint.[16] The advantage of using a brush with dilute paint is that you can easily wipe away the paint and start over.

Before you start on the canvas itself, consider making study sketches of the scene you intend to paint and use these as reference material for the actual painting. You can also use photographs as the reference material. Make a charcoal outline or an oil monochromatic rendering of the painting before adding color and *make sure the drawing is accurate*. If you start with an inaccurate drawing, the painting process will take longer and the result will most likely be unsatisfactory.

To ensure accuracy, choose any object in the painting that can serve as a unit of measurement in calculating the size of other objects and the space between them. For instance, a common measure of length in figure painting is the length of the head. How long is the body measured in head lengths? How wide is the face measured in eye widths?

The bench could serve as the unit of measurement to calculate the size and spacing of the other objects in the landscape.

Unit of Measurement

---

[16] You should not use a pencil because graphite is not readily compatible with oil paint.

Format: Your first consideration is what overall shape the composition is to have: vertical, horizontal or square. Your answer will determine what format your support (e.g., canvas) should have. Verticals are commonly referred to as "portrait" formats and horizontals as "landscape" formats. Vertical formats tend to draw the eye up which makes them appropriate for portraits as the head is normally located at the top of the picture.

Composition: The arrangement an artist gives to the elements of the painting is called composition or design. Although composition is very personal, there are basic considerations common to all paintings.

- **Abstract design:** When drawing a subject or scene try to discern the underlying *abstract design* of the composition. Try not to recognize the objects in the picture for what they are, for example trees and mountains. Rather look at the objects only as shapes and color masses and then critically examine their relationship to each other in terms of space, light and dark, warm and cool colors, and bright and dull colors. To help you see this, look at your drawing upside down, to make it more difficult for your brain to recognize the objects in the scene for what they are, enabling you to see them more easily as abstractions.

- **Balance**: People feel comfortable when things are in balance. Things out of balance are disturbing. In painting, the balance of the composition is achieved when the impact of all elements in the painting is somewhat equal side to side in terms of size, lights and darks, color intensity and temperature. You can also check the balance of your composition by turning the painting upside down. You will immediately notice if there is a lack of balance and where.

- **Tension**: Too much balance, however, can be boring. Some element of tension is desirable to create excitement or interest. Some imbalance serves the painting. Be aware that today many artists choose asymmetry over symmetry to challenge the viewer and make us aware that our perception of reality today is different than in the past.

- **Focal point**: When someone focuses his sight on an object, things around the object are slightly or largely out of focus depending on their distance from the object. The visual range of our focus is no more than four to six inches, beyond which peripheral vision takes over. Traditionally the artist gives the painting a focal point, which is where the eye is naturally drawn first upon seeing the painting. The objects or areas out of the focal point should not be painted with as much definition or "conspicuousness" as the object(s) in the focal point itself. In landscapes especially, the viewer's eye will likely travel around the painting after resting on the focal point. The artist can plan a path for the viewer, leading him about the painting.

CHAPTER 3 – DRAWING AND COMPOSITION

- **Rule of Thirds:** The focal point need not be in the physical center of the painting, but it ought to be at its conceptual center, drawing the viewer's attention. Locating it slightly off center can create dynamism and encourage the viewer's eye to wander around the rest of the painting. The "rule of thirds" is a long established guide to follow in placing your focal point off center. Divide the image – horizontally, vertically or both -- into three equal parts and position the focal point on or near one of the two imaginary lines of demarcation.

Positive and negative space: Positive space is the area that is contained within the borders of objects in the picture plane. Negative space is the area between forms. Because both types of space involve color mass, both are equally important to the design of a painting.

One can draw an object by following the contours of its positive space or the contours of its surrounding negative space. Checking an object's surrounding negative space is a good way to correct any disproportions you made when drawing its positive space contours. Another way to check for disproportion is to turn the painting upside down or to look at its reverse image in a mirror.

Rule of Thirds:
Place the focal point of the painting on or near one of two imaginary lines that equally divide the image vertically (or as the case may be in landscapes horizontally.) This off-center position gives dynamism to the painting.

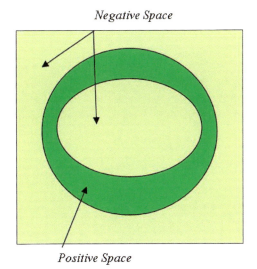

Positive and Negative Space

Oil Painting Principles and Techniques — Lessons of Enzo Russo

Enzo Russo
Girl at the Beach
oil on canvas

Edges: The painter must pay particular attention to the edges of an object as they significantly affect its natural appearance. There are three basic kinds of edges: *hard*, *soft* and *lost*.

- **Hard edges**: Hard edges demark an abrupt break or separation of one object from another. See the illustration below for an example.

- **Soft edges**: Objects with soft edges visually blend to some degree into adjacent space. Clouds are an obvious example of objects with soft edges. In portraiture the lips also should be painted with soft edges.

- **Lost edges**: When the border of one object so completely blends into the border of another object that their point of separation is indistinct, the edges are said to be lost. But this can only happen when the value of the two objects is the same, otherwise the separation is noticeable. A common example of lost edges occurs when the sea blends with the sky under certain atmospheric conditions, obscuring the horizon. Another example is the edge of a dark object blending with an adjacent shadow.

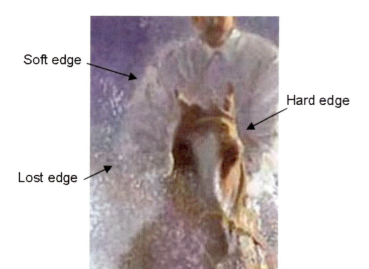

Types of Edges

CHAPTER 3 – DRAWING AND COMPOSITION

Light and Dark

The first consideration in the painting process is the separation of light and dark. The interaction of the two determines the most essential elements in a picture: the form, volume, and placement of the objects. The human brain is "programmed" to see dark shades as receding. Consequently shadows and dark colors help to create the illusion of depth and three-dimensionality.

The Value Scale: "Value" or "luminance" refers to light and dark and their interplay.[17] A color's position on the value scale describes its relative lightness or darkness. Using just white and black paint, you can produce a "gray scale" where the number "9" on the scale signifies pure white (maximum lightness) and the number "1" black (maximum darkness). All of the numbers between measure relative grayness, hence #8 is a very light gray whereas #2 is a very dark gray. The mid-tone gray is at #5.

A painting that has an overall appearance of lightness or brightness is said to be painted in a "high key" whereas a dark painting is said be in a "low key." In a high key painting the darks are close to the lights in the value range; in the low key, the lights are close to the darks. These narrow value ranges can create an overall "mood" in the painting, such as somberness or joyfulness.

Form and Volume

The Illusion of Depth: "Representational" drawing and painting – depicting something as it appears in the real world – are exercises in illusion. Why? Because they attempt to make two-dimensional space appear three-dimensional. One therefore speaks of the "depth" of painting, of its "foreground," "middle ground" and "background." It is as if the canvas were a window through which the viewer sees the actual world.

Perspective: We all know from everyday experience that when a person stands behind another of equal height the one behind appears smaller, provided we, the viewers, are in front of them both. We know that a person's hand when held out to us appears larger than it does when it is at his side. This is known as *foreshortening*, which is the essence of three-dimensionality: *the nearer an object (or part of an object) is to the viewer the larger it appears, and vice versa.*[18] (See "Portrait of a Violinist" on page 36 for an example of foreshortening.)

---

[17] Another technical term in art for the interaction of light and dark is the Italian word *chiaroscuro* [pronounced "kiaroskuro."]

[18] In ancient Egyptian painting, which was two-dimensional or flat, the relative size of a person in the picture plane indicated not his or her *spatial* position but his or her *social* or power position in that culture.

It was not until the Renaissance that artists figured out the rules of approximating perspective in painting. They realized that not only does an object appear smaller the more distant it is, it also appears fainter (grayer), less distinct and cooler than it would if it were nearer. The first phenomenon – diminishing size – is called *linear perspective* and the second – atmospheric effect – is called *aerial perspective*.

Linear Perspective: The rules of perspective can be complex depending on the complexity of the scene to be painted, but in essence they are as follows: The height and width of an object diminishes progressively as it approaches the horizon. A classic example of this is railroad tracks between whose rails the viewer stands and sees them converging to a "vanishing point" on the horizon.

One Vanishing Point

The linear perspective of cubic or "volumetric" objects, such as buildings, involve two or more vanishing points. The imaginary extension of the lines defining the top and bottom of each vertical plane (side) of the object converge at separate points on the horizon.

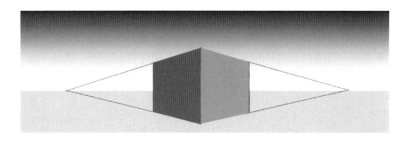

Two Vanishing Points

Three Vanishing Points

Aerial Perspective: Atmosphere causes the appearance of an object to grow steadily fainter, softer, grayer and cooler (bluish or purplish) as you move further from it. The cause is the moisture and dust particles in the air which serve to diffuse and refract the reflected light that bounces off the object before reaching the viewer. The more these particles abound in the air, the greater the diffusion and refraction of light.

CHAPTER 3 – DRAWING AND COMPOSITION

Artists came to realize that in painting an object, such as a mountain, pale (grayish) cool colors push the object back from the picture plane. Conversely, painting an object in bright, highly chromatic and warm colors pulls it toward the picture plane. They also realized that the definition of an object's edges play an important part. Hence:

The warm colors (yellows, oranges and reds) tend to advance
The cool colors (blue, green and purple) tend to recede

Intense (high chromatic) colors advance
Faint (low chromatic) colors recede

Objects with distinct (sharp) edges advance
Objects with indistinct (soft) edges recede

Shadows: Shadows are crucial to the illusion of the three dimensionality of an object (i.e., its volume). To create three-dimensionality, you must understand the **five dynamics of light**: *light* itself, *highlight*, *proper shadow*, *cast shadow* and *reflected light*.

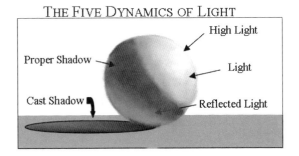

- **Light**: This is the illumination of the object from the light source, such as the sun or a lamp. It is reflected from an object directly to the viewer.
- **Highlight**: A highlight occurs on a curved surface at the point of maximum reflection of light. All other points on the surface reflect slightly less light in the viewer's direction.
- **Proper Shadow**: A proper shadow occurs on those surfaces of an object which are not in the *direct* light illuminating the object.[19] An obvious example is the dark side of the nose in a portrait. The part of a proper shadow closest to the light source appears the darkest.

- **Cast Shadow**: Cast shadows are caused by an object preventing the light from reaching an adjacent surface. An example is a tree's shadow cast across the lawn. Cast shadows are always darker than proper shadows. In the example of the tree, the shadow on the lawn is darker than the dark side of the tree (the proper shadow). A cast shadow is always darkest at the base of the object that is casting the shadow and becomes lighter, less distinct and variable as the shadow recedes from the object because of the additional opportunity for reflected light to impact the shadow.

---

19 Proper shadows are called by some "form shadows" and "natural shadows".

- **Reflected light**: Light bouncing off a surface onto an object is called *reflected light*. Reflected light is important in painting because when it strikes adjacent shadows it makes them lighter. The closer any portion of a proper shadow is to a reflected light source, the lighter that portion of the shadow is. A good example is the bottom half of the dark side of a sphere resting on an illuminated surface – such as a ball on a table bathed in the light of a lamp. The light reflected from the table top strikes the bottom of the ball but not the top, which is out of reach. Thus, the proper shadow at the top of the ball is darker than that towards the bottom.

Enzo Russo
Portrait of a Violinist
oil on canvas, 18"x24"
Notice the five dynamics of light in this portrait. Also, in this painting, the right hand of the violinist and the violin are foreshortened, meaning they move toward the viewer and appear larger.

CHAPTER 4

COLOR

In painting there are fundamentally three levels of color: *primary*, *secondary* and *tertiary*.

Primary colors: There are three primary colors: *yellow*, *blue* and *red*. They are called "primary" because none can be produced from mixing any other colors. All other colors are derivative of the three primaries through their mixture in some combination.

Secondary colors: When two primaries are mixed a secondary color results. Combining red and yellow results in *orange*; mixing red and blue makes *purple* or (synonymously) *violet*; and adding blue to yellow produces *green*. This mixing of the primaries to produce a secondary can occur on the palette, or, as the Impressionists discovered, in the eye of the beholder when two primaries are kept distinct but placed next to each other in a painting which is viewed at a distance.[20]

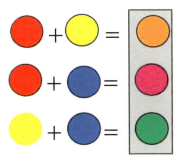

Each of the three secondary colors sits opposite its *complementary* primary color on the "color wheel:"

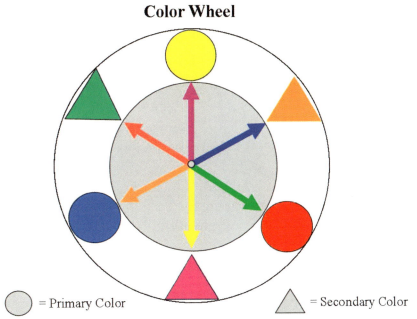

Each of the three primary colors — yellow, red and blue — is located opposite its complementary secondary color on the color wheel.

---

20 This method, known as "optical color mixing," produces a strong color vibrancy,

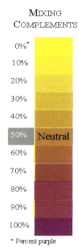

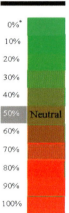

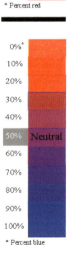

Mixing together two complementary colors (e.g. yellow and purple) reduces their color intensity as shown for the three complementary sets on the left side of this page.

The contrast caused by placing two complementary colors next to each other has the effect of increasing the intensity of each. Hence, green appears greener when placed against red, and vice versa as shown in the illustration on the next page.

Tertiary colors: Tertiary colors are made by mixing all three primary colors or by mixing a primary color with a secondary color that is *not* its complement. This is how the so called "earth colors" are produced: ochres, siennas, and umbers. If colors are indiscriminately mixed they may appear muddy. Paint becomes "mud" when it is no longer identifiable as a color. Mud coloring, however, can be useful for certain earthtone objectives and as a contrast to more vivid coloring.

Color Harmony: Color harmony refers to the pleasing interaction between and among colors. Colors that are contiguous on the color wheel are regarded as harmonious, for instance warm, autumn colors like yellow, orange and red or cool, winter colors like blue and purple. A painting with too much color harmony may be boring, so beware.

Properties of Color: There are four properties of color important to painting: *hue, value, temperature* and *chroma*.

- **Hue**: "Hue" is synonymous with "color." It defines the "family group" to which a particular color belongs, i.e., blue, red, yellow, orange, etc. Within each group there are endless possibilities of color variations. For instance, within the blue family there are three varieties that commonly have a simultaneous place on a painter's palette: cobalt blue, ultramarine blue and cerulean blue. They differ from one another in terms of value and temperature, which are defined below.

- **Value**: As we have seen, "value" (or "luminance") refers to lightness or darkness. Value is *the most important* property of any painting because it gives form and depth to the objects in the work. In general, colors in their fully intense state differ in value. For instance, yellow has a higher value than its complement, purple. It is more difficult to determine the values of objects when they are in color than when they are in

CHAPTER 4 – COLOR

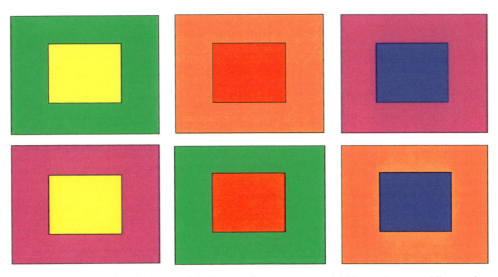

Complementary colors juxtaposed (bottom row) appear more vivid than when apart (top row).

black and white. The best way to do it is to squint, which reduces the amount of light reaching the retina, making the value contrasts more discernable.

- **Temperature**: The "temperature" of a color refers to its *apparent* warmth or coolness. Yellow, orange and red – colors associated with the sun and fire -- appear hot juxtaposed to blue, green and purple – cool colors associated with cold and ice. The former are therefore called warm colors and the latter cool colors. However, any two colors in the same hue can also have differing temperatures. For instance a green mixed with a tad of yellow is warm compared to a green mixed with a bit of blue. Indeed, color temperature is always relative. A cool color can appear "warm" next to a cooler color, or cool next to a "warmer" color. *The impression we have of an object's color, value and temperature is dependent on what is located near or next to it on the canvas.*

- **Chroma**: The "chroma" of a color refers to its intensity. A color's chroma is at its maximum when that color has *not* been mixed with any other, including white and black. You can diminish a color's chroma by deliberately mixing it with another color, especially its complementary color. Low chroma colors appear to recede from the picture plane whereas high chroma colors appear to advance.

White and Black: White, emitted light is the full mixture of all the prismatic colors. Black is the total absence of light. With paint however, which only reflects light both white and black are distinct colors and are often mixed with another color to alter their value, temperature or chroma.

White paint is used to tint a color, that is to make it appear lighter.[21] Simultaneously it also makes the color cooler and grayer. Black has the same side effects when used to darken a color, i.e., changing its shade. Unlike white, black can alter its hue when mixed with yellow, turning it into a green. Because of their "side effects," Enzo Russo recommends that you not use black or white alone to effect a value change in a particular color. You must also mix in other colors to maintain the original color's temperature and chroma. There is no formula for this. You must learn by doing and experiment.

Some painters banish the color black from their palette. Enzo Russo, however, gives black a place on his palette but never uses it alone. He finds that a little touch of black is effective in knocking down the chroma of a color and it can be used in combination with other colors to achieve certain effects.

Color and Shadows: Shadows have color due to the color of the underlying object—its "local color"—and due to the effect of reflected light impacting the shadow. Shadows are not just dark spots. Give them color! Beginners often paint shadows as a uniform black or neutral dark value. Shadows contain a variety of colors, both "local" and reflected. Well painted shadows are important to a quality painting. It is important to note that there is an area of redness at the point where the light meets a shadow, due to the refraction of the light. Rembrandt was the first to observe this physical effect.

Thick and Thin: Rembrandt also discovered that thick paint applied to light areas catches and reflects more light, including highlights, resulting in more brilliance than would be the case if the paint were thin and flat. He found that the grooves of brush strokes are more apparent in light paint than dark paint because the grooves' shadows are more evident. He discovered that visible brush strokes have greater appeal than a flat surface. Painters have exploited his discovery ever since.

Parenthetically, Enzo points out that the development of thick paint had a revolutionary effect on the economy of art. It enabled artists to complete their paintings many times faster than when they had to rely on liquid paint. The Old Masters' method was to use many coatings of glazing over the first base. Each coating of course required a greater amount of time to dry, greatly lengthening the time required to complete the painting. Realizing that using less oil produced a thicker paint, artists were able to circumvent the multiple glazing method to achieve the same effect. Consequently they were able produce many more works than earlier artists. The supply of paintings grew and consequently their market price dropped, making it possible for commoners (merchants, tradesmen and others) to own them. This democratization of art grew even more widely and rapidly when in the mid 19th Century factories began manufacturing ready-made paint contained in tubes. This tubed paint enabled

---

21 Enzo Russo recommends *titanium* white for color mixing.

artists to venture out of their studios to paint in the plain air, which became the common practice of the Barbizon School and the Impressionists.

Highlights and Glare: There is a distinction between a highlight and a glare. A *glare* is a reflection of the total amount of light reaching a surface. Because glare is essentially colorless it occasions the one exception where you can use pure white in a painting. A *highlight*, on the other hand, has the color of the underlying surface where it most directly faces the light source, conferring the highest value. Highlights are generally painted last under the principle of painting "dark to light," and they usually add the biggest impact to the appeal of the painting. The highlights "light up" the painting, creating intensity, contrast, volume, warmth and excitement. Because of their power, use highlights sparingly.

Dynamic Grays: When most people think of gray they think of a dull mixture of black and white. In painting, however, the word "gray" most often refers to color. Gray colors result from the mixture of two complementary colors plus white, or the mixture of the three primary colors plus white. Gray colors play an essential role in almost every genre and style of painting. Gray tones acquire the important role of enhancing the natural hue of the colors next to them. Matisse, for example, frequently used gray as a color enhancer to bring out the chroma quality of the adjacent colors.

Transparency: Some paint pigments are more opaque or more transparent than others. For instance, alizarin crimson, a cool red paint, is more transparent than cadmium red, a warm red. Hence alizarin is good for glazing over another color but not very good for masking it.[22] By using the various paints you will become familiar with the relative transparency of each. Experiment by swabbing them onto bright white paper that has a dark line drawn down the center to see how much of the underlying white shines through and how hidden the line is. You will find that transparency varies by brand, manufacturer and price.

"Permanence" (or "light fastness") is another chemical aspect of paint pigment. This has to do with the ability of the paint, once dry, to withstand fading from exposure to light over time.[11]

The Artist's Palette: The word "palette" refers to three things in painting: first, the physical object on which you place and mix your paints; second, the particular choice and arrangement of paints an artist places on the palette; third, the recurring colors found in an artist's paintings over time. Here we refer to the second meaning.

---

[22] Because of the wide assortment of commercially produced oil paints that are permanent or lightfast you should avoid paints that are not. Look on the face of the paint tubes for the rating the American Society for Testing and Materials (ASTM) has given to that particular paint. ASTM I signifies excellent light fastness, ASTM II equates with very good light fastness and ASTM III signals that the paint is not sufficiently lightfast.

Keep in mind that one cannot buy tubes of paint which are the pure primary colors from the color wheel. One purchases tubes of paint produced from various pigments by a variety of manufactures. These individual paint pigments actually include multiple hues even though one predominates, placing it in a particular color family. For instance, the illustration below shows five common paints in the blue family. Each has characteristics that differ from the others. Cerulean is a warm blue green color and is opaque. In contrast, French Ultramarine is a cooler blue violet color and is transparent. This array of blues gives the artist many choices to best achieve his particular painting objectives.

Enzo Russo recommends a complete array of colors on the palette as this affords greater convenience and versatility in mixing colors. He says that for a minimum you should have for each of the major hues a warm and a cool color version, for instance a lemon yellow (green-yellow) and a cadmium[23] yellow (orange-yellow). Enzo Russo recommends three values for each of the primary hues (e.g., a light cadmium red, medium cadmium red, and a dark cadmium red) as this helps avoid the problem of adding white or black to change the color's value with the unwelcome consequence of also changing temperature and chroma.

From left to right:
Cerulean blue (a warm light greenish, opaque blue)
Phalo blue (a warm greenish, transparent blue}
French ultramarine blue (cool violet, transparent blue)
Cobalt blue (cool, slightly violet blue)
Prussian blue (very dark violet blue)

---

[23] "Cadmium" refers to the type of metal used in the pigment.

CHAPTER 4 – COLOR

Enzo's Palette

Enzo Russo generally has on his palette multiple colors of the three primaries – yellow, red and blue; and fewer for the secondaries – orange, green and purple. He also has readily at hand on his palette certain tertiary (brown or "earth tone") colors – raw umber, burnt umber and burnt sienna. Grouped in with the yellows are ochre and raw sienna. Finally, he dollops out generous portions of titanium white and a small amount of lamp black. Enzo Russo arranges these colors on his palette in the following clockwise progression: lights to darks, warms to cools, starting on the left hand side of the palette. Make sure you have placed all of the paints on the palette *before* you start painting and be generous in the amount of paint you dole out.

If you want to produce your secondary colors – orange, green and purple – by mixing the primaries – blue, red and yellow – be aware that you will need to have a cool and warm version for each of the primaries on your palette:

> for red you will need *cadmium red* and *alizarin crimson*
> for blue, *cerulean* and *ultramarine*
> for yellow, *cadmium yellow* and *lemon yellow*

Cadmium red has a touch of orange, while alizarin crimson has a hint of purple, making it the cooler red. Cerulean has a bit of green making it warmer than ultramarine blue which has a bit of purple. Similarly cadmium yellow has some orange (warm) whereas lemon yellow has some green (cool).

Double Primaries and Secondaries

The most vibrant secondary colors are made when primaries with traces of the desired secondary color are mixed. Hence, the most brilliant green occurs when lemon yellow, containing a trace of green, is mixed with cerulean blue, which also contais a trace of green. It is the same with purple or violet by mixing alizarin crimson with ultramarine blue, which both have traces of purple or violet; and with orange by mixing cadmium yellow with cadmium red, which both have traces of orange.

Mixing primaries with trace colors other than the resultant secondary produces a relatively dull or gray secondary color. This is because the trace color in at least one of the two primaries is from the third primary, and, as we have seen, mixing the three primaries produces grays and earth colors. Hence, for example, a dullish, grayish green occurs when cadmium yellow (with a trace of orange-red) is mixed with ultramarine blue (with traces of purple-red), red being the third primary color.

CHAPTER 4 – COLOR

Enzo Russo
America
oil on canvas 52" x 60"

Oil Painting Principles and Techniques — Lessons of Enzo Russo

Smoke, Beer and Erotik Politik II
Oil in canvas 70x46"

Queen of the Night
Oil on canvas 70x46"

Not so Intimate Voices
Oil on canvas 70x46"

Enzo Russo's *Cabaret* Series

Enzo Russo did a series of five large oil paintings on the theme of the cabaret, emblematic of the Weimar Republic in Germany between World War I and World War II. The importance of the cabaret, he explains, resided in the fact that it was the major gathering point for artists and intellectuals at that time.

Smoke, Beer and Erotik Politik I
Oil on canvas 70x46"

Star of the Night
Oil on canvas 70x46"

CHAPTER 5

CONCEPTUAL PRINCIPLES

Being Painterly: The practice of the Old Masters was to paint by *glazing*, applying successive overlays of dilute, transparent paint, producing a smooth glossy surface with astonishing depth.[24] Often they made color sketches of their subject matter using oil paint. These sketches were done with free brush strokes which were very evident. This manner of clearly showing brush strokes grew in appeal over time and became known as "painterly." *Ala prima*, when the painting is started and completed in one session, is an example of the painterly technique. So is *impasto* painting, where the paint is applied in a particularly thick manner.

Enzo Russo encourages all of his students to adopt this "painterly" style of evident brush work, reminding them that a painting is not a photograph. He respects photography as another art form, but it is not painting. He also points out that a photograph includes every detail present in a scene whereas a painting should only include those details which are essential. He urges us to strive for simplicity, keeping only those details that advance the concept of the painting.

Concept is the intent of a painting. It is the "message" the artist means to convey to the viewer. In contemporary art, Enzo Russo notes, a painting's concept has emerged as the most important consideration, even more so than its style and technique. An artist's technical abilities are quite secondary to his delivery of the concept of his painting. He or she knows that rules of painting are essential guidelines helping them deal with technical matters. They also know that the creative imperative can cause them to go beyond the rules, breaking them when necessary to achieve their concept.

Although every painting should start from a clear concept, in the process of executing the work something in the painting that was not planned or foreseen frequently happens. If this unanticipated development "works" – i.e., enhances or even changes the direction of the painting for the better – recognize it as such and exploit it to the advantage of the painting. Look for clues that tell you where the painting wants to go and be prepared to follow it.

Contrast and Variation: These have to do with varying the basic elements of painting: composition, hue, value, chromatic intensity, temperature, texture, brushwork, etc. Placing primary colors against their secondaries, warms against cools, darks against lights, high against low chroma, curved lines next to straight ones, and so on, creates vitality and interest, the visual equivalent to musical variations and counterpoint.

When painting a large area of a single color, don't be like a house painter who rolls paint uniformly onto a wall, showing no variation or contrast. Rather add in other colors

---

24 Twenty or more layers were not a uncommon practice.

Oil Painting Principles and Techniques Lessons of Enzo Russo

Eline de Jonge
Shadows Grand Central II
oil on canvas, 48"x48"

Shadows of New York
A Series of Oil Paintings by Eline de Jonge

Eline de Jonge
Shadows Grand Central III
oil on canvas, 36"x36"

CHAPTER 5 – CONCEPTUAL PRINCIPLES

and color attributes without changing the value. In other words, do not mix a great pile of paint to produce a single color before applying it to the canvas. Instead, for every brush stroke mix a small amount using various colors. This way you will get vibrant variations of the principal color.[25] As a rule, remember, no matter the situation you should always alter your color properties.

Motion: Although physically still, paintings can give the illusion of motion. For instance, the effect of wind on tree branches, grass and water can be depicted. People and animals can be made to appear running. (See *Boy in Water* on page 50 for an example.) Although the particular shape and contours of these objects are essential to the appearance of motion (i.e., trees and grass bending, waves braking, animals astride, etc.), the artist's brush work is also determinative of motion. The shape and direction of brush strokes suggest motion, such as rounded strokes for clouds in motion; short, chopping strokes for agitated water; long, bending strokes for waving grass; and so on. One of the most fascinating aspects of van Gogh's paintings is that everything in them seems in motion as a result of his strong, very evident brush work throughout.

Work the Whole Canvas: Be sure to advance the painting in all of its parts *simultaneously*. Don't focus on one area to the exclusion of the others. No portion of the painting should be completed until the other areas have advanced nearly as much. Whatever element of the painting you may be working on must be done in conscious reference to the other elements in every part of the painting: i.e., hue, value, chroma, temperature, shapes, perspective, edges, etc. To get any of these right in one part of the painting you must compare it to what is happening in the other parts. So, be sure to "work the whole canvas."

Painting from Photographs: The camera has become a valuable tool in art. Most artists to some degree use photographs as an important reference. When you are painting from photographs keep in mind that the camera records a limited value scale, from about 3 to 7. Brighter values tend to appear washed out and, similarly, darker values look blacked out, while real life has great color variation and interest within these lighter and darker areas. Paint these areas not as recorded by the camera but as they are in real life. Translate the language of photography into the language of painting.

Copyright Issues --- Painting from Another's Photograph:

If you are painting from a photograph not taken by you, remember that the photographer is the one with the copyright interest in the photo image. This means you do not have the right to copy the image, or reproduce the image in a manner that is "substantially the same". Creating art from another's work is referred to as a *derivative work*. In the case of copying a photographic image, you must procure the photographer's permission to do so, which in most cases is not difficult. The right of copyright gives you, the artist creating an original work,

---

[25] All surfaces of varying colors will reflect their hues into the "environment" striking nearby and surrounding surfaces, such as walls.

important rights to your own work as it is created. For an in-depth discussion of painting from a photograph, refer to Appendix B: "Copyright and Other Legal Considerations."

Unity of Style: A good painting has a unity and consistency to its style. Do not mix styles. For example you ought not paint an image half in the Impressionist style and half in the academic, realist style.

Susan Kalla
Boy in Water
oil on canvas, 36"x48"

CHAPTER 6

TECHNIQUES

STANDARD PAINTING TECHNIQUES

While there are many techniques to aid the painting process, there are only a few that you will use on a regular basis. These are discussed below:

Staining the Canvas With an Undertone

You may find it advantageous, especially for portraits, first to paint your canvas with a middle tone color and let it dry. The mid-tone stain allows you to judge more easily the correct values and chroma of the paint you need apply in the initial course of the painting. The brilliant white surface of the primed canvas makes it difficult to make such assessments. The undertone base can also serve to unify the painting, help establish the painting's overall color scheme, or provide a pleasing complement to areas of the over-painting, such as a reddish earth color undertone against green grass. Randomly varying the colors in the undertone affords the possibility of surprising effects that may give you fresh ideas about how to proceed with the painting.

Even if you are painting with oils, consider painting the undertone in acrylic paint, especially if the canvas is large. Acrylic is more economical and dries very fast enabling you to start the oil painting almost immediately.

Wet-on-Wet

The wet-on-wet technique involves applying one wet paint color over another. The result is a soft, amorphous blending of the colors. To achieve this effect, it is important not to paint on a surface that has already started to dry.

Glazing

Glazing is a semi-transparent overlay or wash of one color over another which has already dried. The bottom color shows through and, in the eye of the viewer, mixes with the color of the overlay.[26] The glaze conditions the color underneath. The main purpose of glazing is to modify a color or to give it a vibrancy that is not attained by a premixed color alone. Another purpose is to tone down the chroma or value of an object in the painting.

---

26 Until the early 1500's it was a common practice to paint the skin first in green (a special green called *verdaccio*) and then glazed over many, many times with varying warm skin colors. This created the effect of depth and vibrancy in the skin. Much later, the Impressionists achieved a similar effect by placing on the canvas small daps of different colors which from distance the eye mixes as one single color. Such a method is called the "optical mixture" as distinct from the "palette-mixture" where the various colors are blended before being applied to the canvas.

There are two kinds of glazing: liquid and dry. The liquid approach is the one used by the Old Masters and is still used by artists who prefer the Old Master look. The dry approach is done with the dry brush technique (see below).

Glazing can also change hue. Glazing over one primary color with another will result in a secondary. For instance blue over yellow results in green.

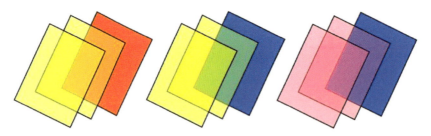

***Glazing** a diluted transparent paint over another paint which has dried works like colored glass. Light passes through the various over-layers, bounces off the bottom strata, and again passes through the top layers only in the opposite direction. The colors of the various layers blend, altering the hue, value and chroma of the bottom layer color, and creating a sense of depth and luminosity.*

Scumbling

Scumbling is similar to glazing in that it involves laying one color over another already dried color. The difference is that scumbling is not done as a wash of very thin, transparent paint but with thicker, more opaque paint rubbed on by a brush leaving bits of the under-paint exposed or peeking through. Enzo Russo recommends using light paint over dark and avoiding dark over light, which causes the paint to look dirty.

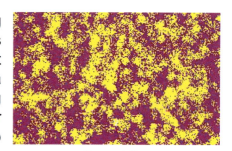

Scumbling

Dry Brush

Dry brush work is also similar to glazing in that it involves applying wet paint over dried paint in a manner that allows the color undertones of the latter to show through the former. The difference again is that the new paint is not thinned or applied as a wash. Unlike scumbling dry brushing involves using a fresh brush with a very small amount of new paint which is not applied randomly, but very carefully and deliberately. Dry brush work is usually done at the very end of the painting process, if done at all. It can be an exhilarating experience to see the great effect such a small amount of paint and so few brush strokes can have in altering the appearance of the painting.

CHAPTER 6 – TECHNIQUES

Blending the Edges of Color Masses

Use a filbert brush to gently stroke, perpendicularly to the joined edge, each color into the other. This is more easily done with oils, with its buttery consistency, than with acrylics.

Cross Hatching

Germano Russo
Pen and Ink Sketch

In drawing, "hatching" is the placement of parallel lines close to each other to create a shade or shadow effect. "Cross hatching" is the same procedure except that another set of parallel lines are drawn or painted across the first group, thereby creating an even darker shade or shadow. The cross hatching technique can also be used with pastel and paint mediums, including oil. It is particularly useful in controlling subtle shadows.

Impasto

"Impasto" is the term given to thick paint. The entire painting can be done in impasto, often with just a painting knife, or the technique can be limited to light value areas. Enzo Russo recommends that the paint in light value areas be thick and that in dark value areas be thinner. Thick paint shows the grooves of the artist's brush work, which is an aspect of the paint surface that is highly valued in contemporary art.

Pattern and Texture

Pattern concerns the ordering of lines, shapes and colors to create a deliberate effect. Texture has to do with the tactile quality of the paint surface. It can be enhanced by the addition of various substances to the paint, such as sand or plaster, or by scraping, grooving or impressing something such as a fork upon a thick paint cover to create an uneven surface. The surface of impasto paintings is also said to be textured.

Rags and Rubbing

Subtle arrays of colors and shades can be achieved by applying paint in a rubbing motion with a small piece of a clean rag.

Use a large canvas

Enzo suggests that you experiment with large canvases, for example 52"x60", because it will provide you with valuable lessons such as putting paint on thickly, developing a free and loose brush stroke, and developing composition on a large format. It will also give you greater confidence. Enzo Russo almost always paints on canvases of this size or larger and often puts two of these canvases together in a mural-like fashion as in the diptych shown below.

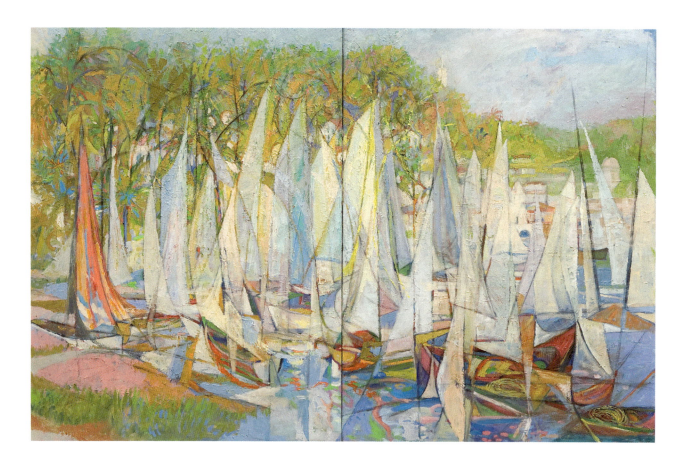

Enzo Russo
Shimmering Sails of Menton
diptych oil on canvas, 48" x 76"

CHAPTER 6 – TECHNIQUES

Techniques for Specific Genres

In addition to the above standard painting techniques, Enzo Russo has given his students many practical pointers concerning techniques germane to specific genres of painting. The following are offered, in turn, for landscape painting, marine painting, still life, and portraiture.

Parenthetically, Enzo Russo notes that the various painting genres that we know today, such as landscapes, still life and portraiture, came into being because of the market forces of supply and demand: the personal preference of artists to a specific subject matter and the art consumers' response to that subject. As the demand for paintings of particular genres increased, artists began to specialize in them and with that came the risk of art becoming commercialized. Resist the temptation of mass producing your art.

<u>Landscape</u>

The following are specific suggestions regarding landscape painting.

Sky

- The sky generally becomes progressively lighter as it approaches the horizon. This is due to the sunlight reflected from the surface of the land back into the sky. This effect is not as apparent at dawn or dusk because of the position of the sun near the horizon.
- For blue skies lightly tint the area just above the horizon with orange.
- A good color mixture for blue skies is cobalt, ultramarine blue and titanium white with a pinch of black. The black is used to reduce the chroma of the blue. Use more ultramarine blue in the apex of the sky than elsewhere. Don't apply the paint uniformly; on the canvas show a mix of colors, including hints of cerulean blue, which is a warm blue for temperature contrast, plus bits of green and violet. Make your brush work apparent.
- When painting clouds establish color contrasts. Don't just use white; add touches of blue-grays and violets (cool colors) contrasted with ochre and, depending on the atmospheric conditions and time of day, orange and raw sienna (warm colors).
- The underside of clouds is usually dark except in the case of back-lit clouds, which are dark in the center and light on the edges, making a halo effect.
- Be sure to give clouds soft edges.
- Be clear about the cloud types, such as cumulus (massive) and cirrus (thin and wispy). Brush work is essential to creating the sense of cloud motion.

Germano Russo[27]
Tuscan Landscape II
oil on canvas, 36"x58"

Horizon

- Make sure you have the aerial perspective right when painting horizons. They require light cool grays (blues and purples), little definition of objects, and soft edges.
- Make sure the linear perspective is also correct regarding objects in the mid-ground and foreground.

Trees

- Despite conventional wisdom, the bark of trees is never brown. It is almost always some variety of gray.
- Don't attempt to define every branch. Show the trunk and major limbs but only suggest the small bare branches with dry brush strokes.
- Similarly don't attempt to paint individual leaves; instead work with varying color masses that suggest leaves. As always, simplify and soften the edges.
- Vary the greens for contrast and apply ochre and other warm hues for temperature contrast.

---

[27] Germano Russo is Enzo Russo's twin brother.

CHAPTER 6 – TECHNIQUES

Germano Russo
Tuscan Landscape
diptych oil on canvas, 44"x120" 1987

Grass

Don't attempt to paint every blade; simplify by using varying color masses for large areas. Vary the greens and mix ochre and other warm colors. The brush strokes should reflect the vertical direction of the grass.

Water

Reflections in water always have darker lights and lighter darks than the objects being reflected.

Germano Russo
Tuscan Landscape III
diptych oil on canvas, 48"x120"

Marine Painting

Marine painting is a special niche area of the fine arts in which the primary focus of the painting is sailboats and power boats, and this results in certain unique demands and expectations. There is a long established history of marine art dating back to the 1500's.[27] Collectors and producers of this art tend to have experience on the water in boats, which drives their love for this work. Seascapes have some elements in common with marine art, but not the essential ingredient of ships on a body of water as the center of focus.

David M. Renton
Lumber Schooner
The George W. Collins of 1876
oil on canvas, 22"x28"
After a photograph courtesy of Mystic Seaport

---
27 J. Russel Jinishian, <u>Bound For Blue Water</u>, The Greenwich Workshop Press, 2003

CHAPTER 6 – TECHNIQUES

Some of the factors to keep in mind when producing marine art, in addition to the underlying principles and techniques set down previously, are explained below.

Nautical Correctness: It is very important when painting pictures of ships that the painting be nautically correct. That is, the wind and the waves must come from the same direction, the tack and the boat must conform with the wind, the ship character and rigging must be correct, and in general the painting must feel and look believable to a knowledgeable sailor.

Composition: The painting typically should not be a "portrait" of a single ship, unless one decides the ship is of particular importance. Consider including multiple ships, clouds, land mass, buoys, birds, wave structures, and other elements of potential interest, as appropriate, to enhance the effectiveness of the painting. Excellent black and white historic photos to draw ideas from can be obtained from Mystic Seaport (three million images), the Mariners' Museum, the Herreshoff Museum and similar sources. Be sure to take into consideration the copyright issues addressed in Appendix B regarding painting from other's photographs. There is a wealth of photographic subjects available on every waterfront.

David M. Renton
Working Tug D. M. Renton
oil on canvas, 15"x30"

Feel: It is essential to give the feel of motion, water and salt air on the canvas for the painting to be effective. This can be achieved in many ways, including the blown spume, breakers against the hull, sharp heel (mast angle) to the sea or other ships, cutting bow waves and rising wake emphasized with brush strokes.

Painterly: Enzo Russo continually emphasizes the importance of being painterly rather than photographic. Use a camera if you want a photograph. Show the brush strokes with feeling and appropriateness to the natural directions of the mass being painted. Leave out the unnecessary. Provide a sharper image on the focal point than the background. Follow Monet's dictum – put objects in the painting that feel correct but are not identifiable.

Aerial Perspective: Aerial perspective is especially important on the water due to humidity in the air over a distance. Distant land is much lighter and cooler in color (blue and purple) and looses distinctness and chroma.

Ship's Lines: When painting ships, one must be very careful to draw the curves of the hull, sail seams and bending mast accurately. Many marine painters of historic ships make or buy ship models (sometimes made from original ship's plans) and set them in a sand box with the sand modeled with desired wave patterns and shapes. Once the model is set up, light can be shown on it to demonstrate how the sunlight should fall and to determine the proper ship's lines at the established viewing angle. Photography can be useful in this process to record variations and perspectives.

Ship's Curves: Obtain a set of "Ship's Curves" from an art or drafting store. They are similar to French Curves, but longer, and have common ship and sail lines. Hulls, sails and rigging have many curves, which cannot be drawn easily and accurately without a set of Ship's Curves or a similar mechanical tool.

Sails: Sails are almost like faces with beautiful curved surfaces and varied shapes. Sails usually show a degree of warm light translucence in which the sun shines through the backside of the sail fabric. Cast shadows often fall from one sail onto another creating an opportunity for light/dark value contrasts. Proper shadows on the sail surfaces create sail volume and enhance the impression of sail shape. Sunlight reflecting off the sail is a warm bright white, in contrast to the same sail material in shadow, which can be much darker and cooler. Consider a soft rose transition between the light and dark of the proper shadow on the sails, an effect discovered by Rembrandt in portraiture. The sails contain a great amount of detail including shape, shadows, seams, imperfections, translucence, bolt ropes, reefing points, grommets, battens, registration numbers, blocks, running lines of all kinds, and much more. One needs to decide how much detail to include and how much to leave out. Often less detail yields a more effective impression.

Rigging: Rigging can be painted with thin rigger brushes (having extra long bristles to hold paint), drafting pens, or a flat brush with a carefully crafted thin edge. "Ship's Curves" are very helpful in drawing these lines. The thin lines also need to demonstrate light, shape, color, shadow and texture. Rigging paint must be thinned with medium in order to lay down a thin line. Enzo Russo suggests using colored pencils as an alternative to paint for rigging.

CHAPTER 6 – TECHNIQUES

When the pencil lines are partially covered with surrounding paints and then the painting is varnished or waxed the pencil lines can become very believable rigging.

Wave Structures: Waves should be drawn and painted with the same detail as the ships. Add a lot of color in your water, to provide interest. Include greens, grays, violets, and of course all the reflected colors from the surroundings including ships sails. The surface behind the waves reflects the light blue sky, while in contrast the front side of the rising wave shape at a stepper angle does not reflect the sky and is therefore darker. Waves rise to a sharp hard edge on top and have a lost edge on their bottom. Waves collect into groups with both variation and consistency, and they always come generally in the same direction as the wind since they are created by the wind. Waves are not uniform. They tend to have more mass on one end than the other. The white foam at the top of a wave has lighter and darker areas depending on which part is directly in the sun and which is shaded. The wind often blows a light spray off the wave that is important to capture with a dry brush technique after the underlying paint has dried to give the feel of wind and motion.

Enzo Russo and David Renton
Schooner Alberta
Oil on Canvas 20"x24"
After a photograph courtesy of
The Mariner's Museum, Newport News, VA

Sea Types: Dead calm seas can make an interesting painting. This glassy languidness must be consistent throughout the painting. As the wind increases, and in turn the waves, the boat's heel and the motion of the waves change the feel of the painting. Very rough seas can result in dramatic and effective paintings, perhaps the most popular. The tension created by large waves and contrasting mast angles transmit the feeling of great force. The power of ships bashed by large, dangerous waves covered in flying spume may yield an especially compelling composition.

Rose Effect: Enzo Russo suggests incorporating a dry brushed rosy late afternoon sky on the horizon setting a feel of warmth contrasted against the cool water and blue sky to enhance the impact of the painting.

Still Life

The term "still life" refers to painting an arrangement of inanimate objects. Unlike in landscape painting, the artist chooses what objects make up the painting, how they are arranged and how they are illuminated. All of these choices are integral to the creative process and often as challenging as the painting process itself.

You can make interesting still lifes almost with any assortment of things. Make sure that they provide the variety necessary for a good painting: i.e., contrasts in value, color, temperature and chroma as well as size and shape. Do not put a great number of objects in the still life. Keep the arrangement simple. Decide which object(s) will be the focal point and arrange it (them) accordingly. Once in place the lighting should not change.

Germano Russo
Flowers and Vase
oil on canvas, 36"x56"

CHAPTER 6

Portraits

In portrait painting, getting the likeness is not enough. The painting must also succeed as a work of art. The two demands have been felt by artists down through the ages, beginning with the ancient Romans. The history of art is replete with great artists who managed both with brilliance: Rembrandt, Holbein, Goya, Velasquez and Sargent to mention only a few. Like them, you should approach portraiture with the principles of great painting fully in mind.

Enzo Russo often recalls Picasso's remark about portraiture: "In the end, a good portrait artist is a caricaturist." He meant that slightly exaggerating the most distinguishing aspects of the subject's face and body helps to capture his or her individuality, character and personality. Get to know your subject, if you do not already. Learn all about him or her in terms of personality, interests, likes and dislikes, favorite activities, clothing style and so on. In deciding how much of the subject's body to include in the painting, base your choice on what is required to capture the activity of the person that best characterizes him or her, as for instance music, gardening, sports, etc.

Enzo Russo points out that for the first time in the history of art portrait artists approach portraiture not as a means of aggrandizing or flattering the subject, but as a honest rendering of the subject's appearance and character, flaws and strengths included. The most knowledgeable client insists that portrait artist paint him or her as the artist *truly* sees him or her. Flattery today is the black beast of portraiture.

With that said and not wishing in any way to constrain or restrict the reader, Enzo Russo offers his students the following pointers regarding the technique of portrait painting. He begins with light.

Enzo Russo
Portrait of Susan Kalla
oil on canvas, 48"x48"

Oil Painting Principles and Techniques — Lessons of Enzo Russo

Enzo Russo
Portrait of a Young Girl
Oil on canvas

CHAPTER 6 – TECHNIQUES

Light
- Strong shadows enhance the impression of volume and three-dimensionality. Therefore, make sure the light illuminating your subject falls across the face and body at an angle so that proper and cast shadows on the face and body are prominent.
- If you chose to use photographs of your subject as reference material, <u>never</u> take the pictures using a flash. The flash washes out shadows and destroys volume. Similarly, do not take photographs of your subject in full sunlight as its intensity causes the lights in the photograph to be so extreme you cannot see subtlety in tones, shades and tints. Rather, take the photo in a soft light such as indirect sunlight or lamp light.
- Be conscious of the light's temperature as it will affect the appearance of the subject. Indirect sunlight and skylight are cool whereas direct sunlight is warm. Lamp light is warm if the bulb has a filament, cool if it is florescent. Try to use a lamp that approximates natural light.

Pose, clothing and props: Give careful thought to the pose you choose for your subjects, the clothes they are to wear, "props" and the background. All of these should be deliberately selected or at least critically approved by you to accomplish the two essential requirements of the portrait: 1) clear expression of the subject's character, personality, profession, favorite activity, etc. and 2) good art.

Proportions of the head: Although the proportions of the face can vary amoung individuals, the following general guidelines are helpful in drawing the proportions of the head.
- The face is divided more or less equally into three areas: forehead, nose and chin. The eyes are located in the center of the head. The mouth is located slightly above the midpoint of the distance between the bottom of the nose and the bottom of the chin. The space between the eyes is equivalent to the width of one eye. The forward contour of the forehead generally casts a partial shadow over the eyes, illuminating the top lid but not the bottom. The ears are located behind the jaw.
- The outer edges of the nostrils align with the beginning of the inner edge of the iris of each eye.
- The corners of the mouth align with the center of the eyes.
- The ears are situated about an inch back from the distance between the top of the nose and the back of the head. The top of the ears align with the eyes and the bottom of the earlobes align with the mouth.

Enzo Russo and Karen Spring
Portrait of a Young Woman II
oil on canvas

This portrait is a demonstration of a combined effort of two artists both bringing their individual talents to bear as was often the case with the old masters and their studio students. Enzo recommends such a collaborative effort as a valuable learning experience.

CHAPTER 6 – TECHNIQUES

Eyes
- Most often the eyebrows are lighter on the side because there is less hair.
- Avoid using pure white for the whites of the eyes. Eyes are usually in shadow and their value and temperature vary according to the angle and condition of the light.
- Because light typically comes from above, the upper eyelid is usually in light and the lower is in shadow.
- Soften the edges of the pupils.
- If you are working from a black and white photograph, for eye and facial shadows you have to "translate" the gray darks in the photo into a recognizable color derived from a red hue, although the color could be ochre in some cases.
- The eyelashes are usually darker towards the end on the outside part of the eye. In some few cases the bottom eye lashes are visible and should be indicated in the painting, especially in the case of women.
- Distinguish between a highlight and a glare. A glare is the reflection of the total amount of light reaching a surface. Because glare is essentially colorless, it occasions the one exception where you can use pure white in a painting. A highlight, on the other hand, has color and occurs on the surface areas of an object most directly facing the light source, conferring the highest value. Highlights are generally painted last (painting dark to light). They usually add the biggest impact to the appeal of the painting. The highlights "light up" the painting creating intensity, contrast, volume, warmth and excitement. Because of their power, use highlights sparingly.

Nose: Never outline the nose on both sides and never shadow the nose on both sides. A shadow on only one side suffices.

Mouth: The mouth is the most changeable part of the face. It is the part of the face that carries 75% of the expression. For that reason many painters find it the most difficult in achieving a true likeness of the subject. [27]

Lips
- For lips generally use orange, alizarin crimson and white. Always apply light over dark.
- Soften lip edges with small perpendicular (vertical) strokes against the edges.
- In the lit area of the lower lip there is a very light pink (especially for women). Use cadmium medium red (cooler than cadmium red light) with a tad of alizarin and white.
- When the light source is from above, the upper lip is in shadow and lower one in light.

---

[27] Enzo Russo tells his students that Sargent is reputed to have defined a portrait as a painting where there is always something wrong with the mouth.

Enzo Russo
Portrait of a Boy
Oil on canvas

CHAPTER 6 – TECHNIQUES

Teeth
- Traditionally artists paint the mouth only with a slight smile, not showing any teeth or very little of them.
- Teeth are never pure white. They are more yellow than white.
- Use a darkish blue base to cool the teeth, then overlay with a yellow brown.
- Do the demarcation of the teeth very gently (no strong lines of separation).
- In the case of an open smile, use a dark for the inside of the mouth: burnt sienna and red.

Skin
- For facial shadows avoid a muddy nameless color. A purple tint lends a cool effect while still providing some red.
- For the temples, the top of the eyebrows and the nose bridge, use ochre (and green, if you are brave).
- There is a blush of red at the edge of a shadow on the face due to the refraction of light.
- Just below the cheek bone the skin is redder than above. This is because the red blood vessels are close to the surface of the skin causing the skin to have a red cast. Use a cool red mixed with the skin color to get the proper effect.
- For the lower cheeks start with a warm color over which lay cool colors.
- Even out color patches to eliminate a spotty appearance. Spotty color patches mostly occur as a result of not having enough paint on the brush. Try to cover the areas where there are shadows and lights with enough paint to eliminate the transparency effect that occurs when the paint is thin.
- For areas of skin in light, lay down a <u>thick</u>, cool under base (using green or ochre); let dry, then dry bush over it a warm color, creating vibrancy and depth.
- Cadmium red mixed with white and a little ochre makes a good cheek color for lighted areas. For women, using alizarin crimson can give the cheeks a cool, peachy look and less the appearance of heavy make-up.
- Cadmium red medium is cooler than cadmium red light; and, cadmium red dark is even cooler. Vermillion (an orange red) is the warmest red.
- Alizarin crimson, the coolest red, is the most powerful red chromatically. Use it sparingly and with great control. That said, it is good for facial shadows for skin that is naturally warm, like cheeks, but always mix it with earth colors – providing a warming balance effect.
- The natural reddish warm color of skin is due to a close proximity of the red blood vessels to the surface of the skin. These areas are typically the end of the nose, the upper portions of the cheeks and tip of the chin.[28] A subdued light color tending toward the ochre is evident in the other areas of the face. A green and/or ochre should be used for skin areas that are naturally cool, such as the temples and areas below the eye sockets.
- When joining cool and warm color areas of the skin, or light and dark areas, always blend from both sides, not just one side into another. As a rule for painting in general,

---

28 The reddish affects are particularly noticeable in British portraiture in the 18th and 19th Century.

when shifting from dark to light on a curved surface, use brush stokes at a right angle from the line of demarcation and from both directions.
- Always soften the edges of proper shadows, but not cast shadows which should have hard edges.
- As always in painting, squint to get an accurate reading of the relative darks and lights. Look to see cool colors in shadows. Since the Impressionists, blue and other cool colors have become synonymous with shadows.
- Laying down warm colors over cool colors helps crate color vibration.

Hair
- Lay down the dark and mid-tone colors first, then the lights. It is always more desirable to use light over dark than vice versa. Dark added over the light generally gives the feeling that the painting is not complete.
- After the basic layout of the dark and light hair masses you should use the side of a small brush filled with lots of paint to draw the stands of hair in a continuous motion from beginning to end.
- Paint the hair soft at the edges where it meets the background so it blends into the background and doesn't look like a cut-out. This can be done by using wet or dry brush strokes.
- For gray hair always use a warm gray, not a cool one.
- For blond hair look for ochre, red and orange tones.

Neck
- The neck area is generally a little cooler than the rest of the face because it less exposed to sunlight.
- It doesn't hurt to add a little extra length to the neck, especially in portraits of women.

Beard
- For dark hair, green-gray or blue-gray is good for beard stubble.
- The techniques that apply to the hair apply to a full beard.

Hands
- Normally, the joints are the thickest and widest parts of the finger. Always taper the finger tips, especially for women.

Background
- The role of the background is to enhance the subject but not to dominate the painting or distract from the subject.
- The choice of background should be made with an understanding of who the subject is and what visual factors contribute to the better definition of his character. Frequently, plain backgrounds work quite convincingly to this end. If you chose to use a plain background be sure to paint it with mixtures of contrasting hues and temperatures while keeping the same value.

CHAPTER 6 – TECHNIQUES

- The Rembrandt effect: Value variation of the background field is also important. Rembrandt invented a value pattern that is very effective and almost universally used ever since in portraiture. He painted the background dark behind the side of the face that is in light, and the light behind the shadow side of the face. Also, he made both the light and dark sides of the background grow gradually lighter from top to bottom, similar to the light pattern of the sky.

Enzo Russo
Portrait of an Equestrian
oil on canvas

Enzo Russo
Balancing Act on Marshall Street
oil on canvas, 48"x73" 1996

CHAPTER 7

THE PAINTING PROCESS

The painting process involves more than just the application of the principles and techniques of painting reviewed in the previous chapters. There is also a logical sequence of steps you should follow: first, plan your painting; second, draw the composition and block it in; third, add and refine the detail; and lastly, know when it is complete.

Plan your painting

You should be clear about what it is you want to paint and why. What motivated you to choose the particular subject, composition and treatment you have in mind. What is the underlying *concept* of the painting, the ideas and feelings you wish to express (i.e., the "message")? This is the most important consideration, as mentioned earlier, because it determines the aesthetic direction you opt to follow in doing the painting and assures that you will not be painting aimlessly.[29] Name your painting to focus your concept.

When making these choices, Enzo strongly advises that you avoid sentimental subjects and treatments, commonly associated with picture postcards and calendars, such as sunsets. The viewer expects your painting to reflect you and your desires, creativity and imagination.

Decide if you are going to start and complete the painting in one session (*alla prima*) as is often the case when painting a landscape outdoors (*en plein air*), or if you will do the painting in stages in your studio.[30] If the latter, you may want to do preliminary sketches and take photographs as reference material. If you are painting from a photograph, study it well. Closely examine the composition and the patterns of light and dark (the relative values of the parts). *Learn how to read photographs correctly if you rely on them for your subject matter!*

Analyze the perspective elements of the picture. Is there one or more vanishing points? Determine the horizon line and place the vanishing points in their correct positions.

Decide what is to be the center of focus. Also determine what is non-essential in the composition and eliminate it in order to *simplify* the composition and thereby strengthen the painting and make it more painterly. Remember, less is often more.

Determine the light source in the picture, how cool or warm the light is, and how it flows across the composition.

---

[29] Every art work should start from a clear idea or concept. However, in the process of executing the work something in the painting that was not planned or foreseen frequently happens. The painting may be giving you clues as to where it wants to go that you had not anticipated. At that point you must be prepared to follow the clues. Do what the painting requires.
[30] If, as an economy measure, you decide to paint over a used canvas, you should sand the surface of the old paint to remove enough of it to allow the new paint to grip the underlying fibers without damaging the fibers.

Draw the composition using either charcoal or thin, diluted paint (preferably an earth color) or by directly painting in the major color masses. It is important to paint masses and shapes of color, rather than outlines. Save yourself from frustration and trouble later by avoiding having to undo, late in the painting process, your early initial drawing mistakes!

"Block in" the painting

Once the drawing is complete and accurate begin blocking in the color masses. Paint the dark areas first, then the mid-tones and lastly the lights. Squint to get a correct reading of values and edges.

Paint from the background to the foreground: sky, background, middle ground, and foreground. Paint dark to light putting highlights in last. Whenever painting a "dark" make sure it's filled with color. Put in big shapes first, then fill in small shapes. Work from broad impression to detail.

For both speed and economy you can use acrylic, which are cheaper than oils, to block in your painting and then finish it with oils. (Note: Although you can cover acrylic paint with oils, you should not do the reverse because the acrylic will not adhere.)

Susan Kalla
Block-in for Oil Painting on Canvas
Pool Series

CHAPTER 7 – THE PAINTING PROCESS

Refine the painting

Once you have blocked in the painting you should let it dry to the touch before beginning the process of putting in the details and otherwise refining the painting. As you progress into the refinement phase of the painting, keep in mind the following advice from Enzo Russo:

- Don't be preoccupied in completing any one section before going on to the next. All parts of the painting should advance simultaneously.
- As you paint, work to simplify.
- When joining cool and warm color areas and light and dark areas always blend from both sides, not just one side into another. As a rule for painting in general, when shifting from dark to light on a curved surface use brush stokes at a right angle from the line of demarcation and from both directions.
- Create contrasts to enrich the painting and create interest:
    - Warm and cool
    - Hard, soft and lost edges. In soft edges, use brush strokes perpendicular to the edge.
    - Light and dark values
    - Dramatic color hues and grayed-out colors
    - Complementary colors
- Create depth using these techniques:
    - Check for correct linear perspective
    - Include the atmospheric effects of aerial perspective
    - Light values advance, dark values recede
    - High intensity colors advance, low intensity colors recede
    - Warm colors advance, cool colors recede
    - Define your foreground, mid-ground and background
    - Objects in the focal point are in sharper focus than objects outside the focal point, especially distant objects
    - Overlapping objects appear to advance, while overlapped object appear to recede
- Give color content to the shadows – make them interesting.
- Add reflective light, which is always cooler and darker than direct light.
- Paint light colors thickly and paint dark colors thinner.
- Never hesitate to paint with lots of colors.
- Break down the uniformity of a color area into the color components of that area.
- Show painterly brush strokes. Hold your brush correctly: high on the handle and flat to the canvas.
- If you made a mistake and find that it works, leave it alone
- Keep the style consistent: detailed throughout, impressionistic throughout, etc. Don't mix styles.

Know when to stop: At some point your painting is complete, a point beyond which further effort could very well ruin it. Enzo Russo says that when he was a student in Florence the class spent two hours discussing this question. The answer they found is that a painting is complete when the underlying concept is complete, or, in others words, when you have said all that you had intended to say. Remember, a good and complete painting involves the deliberate *exclusion* of things.

Eline de Jonge
Shadows & Light Grand Central
Oil on Canvas, 48"x48"

AFTER THE PAINTING IS FINISHED

Once you have finished your painting and it has dried sufficiently there are four further steps you might consider taking: signing it, protecting it, framing it, and photographing it. This chapter gives advice on each of these.

Signature

Enzo Russo recommends that you write your name on the painting as you normally sign any document in order to establish authenticity. Don't use a color that makes your signature conspicuous, but do regard it as part of the painting. Consider using a pencil or even signing your name on the back of canvas. Enzo Russo also recommends that you emboss your thumb print next to your signature to reinforce your authorship of the painting. Enlarge your thumb print and give it to your gallery or agent so he or she can authenticate paintings signed with your name.

Peter S. Robinson
Block Island
Lighthouse
oil on canvas, 22"x28"

Protecting your painting with wax

Although Enzo strongly disagrees with the practice, many artists apply some kind of varnish to the surface of a painting after it has thoroughly dried for at least six months or more. In addition to protecting the painting surface from dust, dirt and pollution, varnish tends to enhance the "richness" of the colors. Varnish can be applied as a spray or as a liquid brushed on. The traditional varnish for oil paintings has been damar, a natural resin, either applied alone or mixed in some combination with linseed oil and or turpentine. The drawback with damar varnish is that it will yellow and darken over time and crack. To help compensate for this, stabilizers are often added to the varnish. There are now synthetic varnishes on the market which, it is claimed by their manufactures, do not yellow or deteriorate with age. However they may have a plastic like sheen which some artists find unattractive.

The best way to protect the painting, Enzo emphasizes, is to wax and buff it using the following technique. The wax will, like varnish, enrich the colors, but it will not darken, yellow or crack. To apply wax, make sure the painting is dry (at least four weeks after finishing). Place the painting on a flat surface. With a clean cloth apply a high quality wax such as Renaissance Wax developed and approved for manufacture by the British Museum.[30] Do not apply the wax too thickly or too thinly. Common sense will guide you in putting on a proper coat of wax. Let it dry for two or three days. You can tell when it is dry by buffing a corner of the painting with a clean soft white cloth. If the buffing brings up a shine, it is dry, if not it is not yet dry. Then repeat the same process with a second coat of wax. After the second coat is dry, if a gloss is desired, buff lightly by hand with a clean white soft cloth until a nice shine is evenly distributed across the face of the painting. The buffing is made easier with an inexpensive six-inch orbital electric hand buffer having a soft disc cover.[31] Use the electric buffer very carefully and gently so as not to harm the painting. This process will create a glossy rich protection over the paint that will not crack or melt and will last for many years. When buffing, be sure to avoid pressure on the stretched canvas by supporting the underside of the canvas on a flat surface, such as a stack of magazines built up just to the level of the fabric. The wax may be readily removed in the future when and if desired by careful application of mineral spirits or turpentine on a clean soft white cloth. You will find this waxing process quite easy to apply after just a little practice. [32]

---

[30] Renaissance Wax can be purchased from Wood Finish Supply, 800-245-5611 or www.woodfinishsupply.com//RenWax.html, or other suppliers.
[31] For example the Ryobi can be obtained at Home Depot.
[32] According to Ms. Dianne Modestini of the New York University Department of Conservation many artists have preferred wax such as Gauguin and Andrew Wyeth.

CHAPTER 8 – AFTER THE PAINTING IS FINISHED

Framing

The function of a picture frame is to separate the image from the surrounding space,[33] thereby "setting it off." The color, style and size of the frame should be chosen to complement the specific qualities of the painting. Custom made frames are best but usually are quite expensive. Fortunately most discount art supply stores have an assortment of readymade ones in varying sizes at much lower cost. They also sell assembly pieces with which you can make your own frame.

Are frames really necessary? Many people today prefer no frame and use canvases that are tacked or stapled on the back, leaving the sides free for painting. Enzo's view about frames is to use them sparingly. "Don't feel that you have to frame everything," he notes. For small to medium size paintings Enzo Russo recommends large mattes (3-4 inches wide) and a moderately small and simple molding. In all cases the frame should not compete with the painting, only complement it. Finally, Enzo Russo warns that a bad frame can ruin the effect of a good painting.

Photographing your painting

It is recommended that you keep a photographic record of your work (see Appendix B). This can be done simply using a point-and-shoot digital camera. The image produced will be in the "jpeg" format which digitally compresses the image making it very suitable also for website posting.[34]

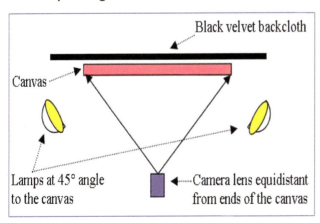

If, however, you want to make high resolution prints of your work for publication and for a professional record (requiring a minimum of 300 dpi[35]) you will need to use an SLR (single-lens-reflex) camera capable of manual adjustment. You will also need a sturdy tripod on which to place the camera to prevent it from shaking, even slightly. A shutter release cable or self-timer feature built into camera is a further means of keeping the camera from shaking.

---

33 Another useful purpose of a frame is to cover the sides of the canvas where the tacks or staples anchoring the cloth are visible. This need is obviated by buying canvases where the stapling or tacking is done on the back, allowing the sides to be painted and made part of the picture.

34 The reason jpeg pictures are suitable for websites is that their compression -- relatively small amount of digital information, or bytes – makes their down load from the internet relatively fast. People with a "dial-up" internet connection would have to wait a long time for high resolution pictures to down load, testing their patience.

35 A minimum of 300dpi is required for publication and printmaking purposes. DPI (dots per inch) is a printing term. PPI (pixels per inch) is a digital photography term.

For indoor shooting, you will need two tungsten photoflood lamps model 3200k, (250-500 watts[36]) in silver reflectors which are positioned on either side of the painting at a 45 degree angle. You will also need to hang a black velvet cloth evenly draped behind the painting. The painting should be suspended vertically and the camera position in front of it with the lens equidistant from each side of the painting and from the top and bottom edges – that way it will be perfectly centered. If the painting is not centered perfectly its shape will appear distorted, more like a trapezoid than the square or rectangle it should be. In the photograph, the corners need to be at true right angles as they are in reality.

If the painting is framed, remove the frame so you can screw two eye hooks into the top part of the support to which you attach strong black threads to suspend the painting. That way the painting will hang in true vertical angle. Make sure the top edge of the support is completely horizontal. Use a carpenter's balance. Also, it is better to photograph the painting before it is waxed or varnished, as both can cause a sheen and reflection that compromises the image quality.

For indoor shooting with a film camera you should use a professional tungsten slide film, such as Kodak's Ektachrome 64T. If you opt for the digital camera you will need to set its white balance to "tungsten."

The above rules for positioning the painting, camera and backdrop also apply to the outdoors.[37] If you prefer to photograph the painting outdoors, do so in an open shade in the late morning when the sunlight color balance is most even. Use a daylight filter and a *slide* film such as Kodak's Ektachrome 64.

Now the burning question is, should you use a *film* or *digital* SLR camera? Film cameras are easier to use than digital cameras in as much as there is no need to use a computer to process the image to get it right. Film is also sharper and able to accommodate a larger color range than digital cameras, save the high end professional ones.

You can digitalize film slides by taking them to a camera shop capable of scanning them (or by acquiring a slide scanner for yourself). Once they are digitalized you can crop and otherwise alter them in your computer using photo-editing software.[36] More importantly you can convert them to the jpeg format for purposes of website posting and gallery and exhibition submissions. And you can also convert them into high resolution images needed for publication, printmaking, and documentation purposes.

---

36 Make sure the lamp socket is porcelain, capable of handling high wattage.
37 The backdrop or background can be cropped out of the photograph when digitalized, using a photo processing computer program.

CHAPTER 8 – AFTER THE PAINTING IS FINISHED

Digital cameras have the advantage of producing instant and cost-free images endlessly, which allows you to shoot dozens if not hundreds of pictures with no out-of-pocket expense. With so many shots you are bound to get one that is just right.

Images produced by digital cameras may require "tweaking" (digital adjustment) with the computer to render the colors and values true to your painting. Complicating the process is the fact that computer screens vary widely in quality and calibration for colors and values. So you have to compare what you see on your computer screen with your painting, holding the one near the other, and make the necessary adjustments accordingly. This comparison is facilitated by placing a gray scale and color scale next to your painting when photographing it, incorporating the two scales in the picture.[37] You can then adjust the digital image by comparing the gray and color scales on the screen with the actual ones in your hand.

The manual adjustments to both types of cameras in setting up the shot are essentially the same – getting the shutter speed and aperture (*f* stop) right in the given light condition. Finding the right exposure setting requires a light meter held before the painting basked in the flood light or outdoor light. Based on its reading you set the *f* stop. The camera can then calibrate the correct shutter speed. (Or the reverse can occur by setting the camera on "shutter priority" which means you set the shutter speed and the camera calibrates the appropriate aperture.)

Having a good camera lens is of critical importance. Inferior ones can distort the image.[12] Although fixed focus lenses produce less distortion than zoom lenses, a quality zoom lens will suffice for our purposes.

There are two other digital image formats that you need to be aware of. One, called "RAW," involves no image compression whatsoever, which means that all of the visual information that the camera takes in is kept in its entirety and no loss occurs with manipulation of the image. Using jpeg, compression information is lost every time a jpeg file is opened

---

36 The most versatile, professional grade photo-editing program (very complex and expensive) is Adobe Photoshop. Fortunately Adobe puts out a much simpler, user-friendly and far cheaper version, called Photoshop Elements, which is capable of doing all that you would want from a photo-editing. Other brands are Corel Paint Shop and Picasa 2 from Google, which has the advantage of being free. (You can download Picasa at www.picasa.google.com.)
37 The scales can be cropped out of the picture when they are no longer needed.
This is another reason not to shoot your picture with a point-and-shoot (instant) camera if the image is meant for publication, printmaking or documentation. Remember, however, because of its compression the jpeg format these cameras use is required for web postings and is quite suitable for snapshot or "family" photographs. Another advantage of jpegs in the website context is that if someone tries to lift the image off the internet to make and market a print the enlarged image will be pretty poor.

and further processed. There is a progressive deterioration in the picture's accuracy and quality. Thus, for high resolution digital photos, it is important to use a camera capable of producing images in the RAW format.

Another file format, called "TIFF," allows for compression but without loss of information. So after a RAW file is processed with photo-editing software it is best saved as a TIFF file. The original image can be kept as a RAW file for backup.

Because of the enormous file sizes of RAW images it is advisable to use a high capacity flash card in your digital camera, a least 1 gigabyte. Also because of the high image resolution required for pictures of your art work taken for publishing, printmaking and documentation purposes, your digital camera should be at least of the 6 megapixel size. You will probably want to store the images in an external hard drive backed up by an additional external hard drive, both of high capacity.

Enzo Russo
Autumn
oil on canvas, 38"x44"

CHAPTER 9

MARKETING YOUR WORK

Artists need tools to take control of their careers and sell their work successfully. It is important to get exposure for your work in order to build up a résumé and to become a successful selling artist. Become a member of your local active art organizations and participate in their juried shows. Also consult art magazines like "Art Times", "Art News", "Art in America," etc. for listings of "call for entry." Research and then make a short list of the galleries you believe have a good fit with your art. Go to openings and network with art people. Once you have established some relations with galleries or with their exhibiting artists (they often rely on recommendations from their artists) you can contact them and ask if you may send them information about yourself.

You only have one chance to make a first impression on a prospective client, gallery owner, curator or art consultant, so it better be a good one. In order to be well prepared, the following items are important;

Theme

It is necessary to develop a theme for your work, so people will start to recognize your art because of its unique style and subject matter. It is essential to choose a theme that is close to your heart and a real source of inspiration to you. Try to find something original that has depth and meaning. It will be easier to write your artist statement once you have found yourself a theme that has that prerequisite. The series should consist of at least 10 or 12 paintings. A full series enhances each individual painting and enables gallery owners or curators to organize a solo-show.

The Artist Statement

The artist statement is a personal description of your work and its meaning. It is important for prospective buyers to read your statement because it is often the only tool they have to fully understand your work, and the way you intended it to be. It is also a promotional tool that can be used in your presentation book, website, exhibition brochure, press kit or application for a grant. Your artist statement also gives you the opportunity to show the seriousness of direction and vision you have. This statement can both be described in writing and expressed orally.

The process of writing the statement also clarifies and fine-tunes your direction and creative goals. It is important to write your own personal statement. There are no strict rules for writing one. You should write it in the first person and keep its length to half a typed page.

Biography

Basically a biography contains the same information as a résumé, but is written in a more enticing paragraph form and in the third person. For a beginning artist it may suffice as a "stand alone" without the connecting official résumé, until you can list more exhibitions, awards, commissions, etc. For the experienced artist, it is used in addition to the résumé. A biography can be used in your presentation book, website and press-kit to emphasize your most important achievements. Parts can also be used for a cover letter to a gallery or museum curator, or as part of a grant application. The biography should read pleasantly and concern your journey through your art career, describing the items listed on your résumé. Don't make it too lengthy. If the biography is short (less than half a page) you may want to include an image of your work.

Résumé

A résumé is the more serious presentation tool and should be up-dated regularly. Use only art related positions in your résumé. Be clear in lay-out and typestyle and use fine quality paper. If your résumé is longer than two or three pages, delete the less important listings and use the phrase "selected exhibitions" and/or "selected commissions."

The résumé should contain the following information:

- Contact data: name, address, phone, email and website
- Place and date of birth
- A list of all the exhibitions, starting with the most recent. If you had various solo shows, list them separately. The same for group and museum shows. Name the jurors and curators of the shows.
- Mention upcoming exhibitions.
- List grants, honors and awards.
- Articles and publications about you, starting with the most recent
- Art related articles or books you have written
- List of commissions with name of the sponsor and location
- Private and public collectors
- Art related activities (teaching, jurying experience, positions in art organizations)
- Membership of art organizations
- Education

CHAPTER 9 – MARKETING YOUR WORK

Preparing your promotional materials

A folder of promotional materials can be used for press releases, shows, and sent to galleries. A full kit includes:

- Business card
- Postcard and or promotional sheet or brochure
- Presentation folder and press kit containing:
    - Artist statement
    - Biography
    - Résumé
    - Photo prints and/or slides of your work in series
    - Publications

Web site

When you design your promotional materials, keep in mind that they ought to be uniform in your choice of fonts, layout, colors and series of featured artwork. In order to get gallery representation it is important to invest time and money in preparing a good presentation that reflects the quality of your work. Today with digital printing techniques it is not very expensive to produce a small number of business cards and postcards. Spend money on working together with a local graphic designer who will make sure that your designs are consistent. This also applies to the web-design. The most effective website is fast downloading so any visitor with either a dial-up or high speed internet connection doesn't have to wait long to see it. The website should be updated regularly. More and more galleries go to the artist's website to view the artwork, instead of using slides.

Finally, consider the legal aspects of marketing your work discussed in Appendix B including formal contracts with your gallery and those who commission your work.

Enzo Russo
Ladies of the Night
Oil on canvas, 18"x24" 1953

CHAPTER 10

CONCLUSION

We conclude this book with a summary of what we believe are the essentials of Enzo Russo's teaching about oil painting. First and foremost be clear as to what you wish to express; that is to say be clear about the painting's concept. Concept is more important than technique. A well executed painting lacking in concept is intrinsically superficial.

Next, appreciate the importance of light in the painting process. Note the temperature of the light illuminating your subject and the temperature of the light illuminating your canvas and palette. Keep in mind that the lights and darks (values) in your painting and their interplay are of utmost importance in the painting process. If you get the values right you will have a good visual result.

Make sure the composition and "drawing" is correct and accurate, including the linear perspective. Do this *early* in the process to save the time and trouble of undoing mistakes later.

Follow the proper sequence of painting: drawing, blocking in the value and color of the background, then laying down the dark tones first, then the lighter ones. Next begin adding detail and refinement. Add only *essential* details, those that are necessary to the concept, eschewing all others. Strive for simplicity, remembering that less is often more.

Be painterly. Put paint on thickly with evident brush strokes. Aim for a textured surface. Vary your bush strokes so they appropriately describe each element in the painting and express your feelings about them. Vary the basic elements of painting: composition, hue, value, chromatic intensity, temperature, texture, brushwork, and so on to create interest.

Invest in quality brushes and treat them with care. Use mostly filberts. Stretch your own canvases if possible, priming them with an acrylic gesso, tinted with an earth tone. Exploit the full range of painting techniques described in earlier chapters.

Develop a portfolio of consistent quality paintings expressing a unifying concept and message. Galleries and collectors are looking not for one good painting, but rather an assemblage of ten or more indicating the artist's consistency in terms of concept and subject matter. Artists zigzagging through various or different subjects and styles are almost inevitably rejected by galleries. They are seeking artists with a personal style and vision. A collection of heterogeneous paintings in various styles and divergent concepts indicates that the artist has not yet found his own "voice."

Stay in touch with the current art scene. Learn what is happening today by visiting prominent galleries and reading current art literature. Especially be attuned to what is going on in the major art capitals. The internet can be very helpful in this process. Be aware that most important galleries today prefer to communicate initially with artists through the internet.

Learn the rules thoroughly, but don't let them handcuff your creativity. Break them where it serves your painting and the concept you wish to express.

Finally, the artist has an obligation to always be reaching for new frontiers. In the words of Enzo Russo, "an artist is always in need of experimentation, of exploring new possibilities, of pushing further and further. When an artist stops experimenting he is finished as a creator and has nothing more to contribute."

Enzo Russo
Cabaret Singer
Oil on Canvas, 70"x46"

CHAPTER 10 – CONCLUSION

Portrait of Young Boy
Enzo Russo
Oil on Canvas

Portrait of William Evarts
Enzo Russo
Oil on Canvas

Eiffel Tower Vision
Enzo Russo
Oil on Canvas
After photographic image
by Robert Wagner

APPENDIX A
ENZO RUSSO BIOGRAPHICAL NOTES

Enzo Russo was born and raised in Florence, Italy. He and his identical twin brother, Germano, attended the School of Fine Arts at the University of Florence. They were admitted two years before the mandatory age of eighteen, after being granted a special dispensation from the Italian Ministry of Education. Enzo Russo went on, after earning his undergraduate degree, to receive a Master's degree in Mural Art. The art school was founded by Michelangelo in the city that was the birthplace of the Renaissance and home of many of history's greatest artists and art works.

Enzo and Germano Russo

Appendix A

As a student in Florence, Enzo Russo was fortunate to have three extraordinary teachers. The first, Ottone Rosai, one of the major Italian artists of that time, had a strong influence in his formation as an artist. Enzo Russo says, "I learned much from him about balancing the strict rules of academic learning with the search for my own direction." The second teacher, Gioavanni Colacicchi, was a living encyclopedia of technical knowledge. His insatiable thirst for learning influenced Enzo Russo's intellectual posture. The third teacher, Giorgio de Chirico, regarded as the father of modern Surrealism, Enzo Russo considers to be one of the two greatest masters of the 20th Century, the other being Balthus. De Chirico was a man of formidable intellect and outstanding intuition. His unique vision strongly inspired Enzo Russo's early work and lighted his way through the perplexing maze of modern art. The two men established a long and close friendship.

After graduating at age 20, both Enzo Russo and his brother moved to Rome to take a one year course in film set design at the "Centro Sperimentale di Chematografia" in Cine Cittá. They were in Rome for a period of four years working on films while simultaneously pursuing their objectives in the fine arts.

Following an award by the Salzburg Seminar for the Arts and Letters, they traveled to Salzburg, Austria, where they made the acquaintance of Pulitzer Prize art historian Oliver Larkin. Deeply impressed with their work, Mr. Larkin, who was the chief moderator of the seminar, sought their friendship and became instrumental in Enzo Russo's coming to America. The following year, Enzo Russo was awarded the prestigious Commonwealth Fund Fellowship in the visual arts becoming the first known foreign artist to receive such recognition.

The purpose of the grant was a cultural tour of the United States following an arranged itinerary which included visiting university art departments and giving a series of lectures about contemporary western European art and art education. An honest and conclusive report on the tour caused an additional year extension of the fellowship. After his research was completed, Enzo Russo stayed on in the U.S. working as a professional artist. Two years later his brother, Germano, joined him.

In 1968, with the sponsorship of the Whitney Museum of American Art, the Guggenheim Museum, the Smithsonian Institution and Oliver Larkin, Enzo Russo received "distinguished foreigner status" and was later accorded American citizenship.

Both Enzo Russo and his brother have been represented by several New York and Boston art galleries.

Enzo Russo presently lives and works in Fairfield County, Connecticut, and teaches at the Studio School of the Greenwich Art Society in Greenwich, Connecticut, and The Painting Studio in Darien, Connecticut. He also teaches a number of private students while pursing his own painting. His work as an artist and teacher has influenced a generation of emerging artists in Connecticut, as well as young artists from all over the world.

Prizes and Awards

- The National Quadrienna of Rome, Italy (at 18 years of age).
- The International Biennale of Venice, (special prize of the President of the Republic to an artist under 21 years of age).
- The Diomira Drawing prize, Civic Museum of Milan, Italy.
- The Michetti Prize, Civitavecchia, Italy.
- "Premio del Fiorino" (National Panoramic, Exhibition).
- Purchase Prize by Marzotto collection.
- First prize from The National Academy of the Art of Drawing (co-awarded with Germano Russo).
- The Salzburg Seminar in American Art Fellowship (co-awarded with Germano Russo).
- Life Fellow member of the Commonwealth Fund Foundation, in New York.
- The Commonwealth Fund Fellowship Grant, after sponsorship by Pulitzer Prize Art Historian Oliver Larkin (a by invitation only award).

Exhibitions in the U.S.

- The World House Gallery, New York, NY
- The Catherine Viviano Gallery, New York, NY
- The Smithsonian institution, Collection of Fine Arts, Washington, DC
- The Contemporaries, New York, NY
- The Rolly-Michaux Gallery, Boston, MA

Enzo Russo
Girl in Chair
Oil on Canvas

APPENDIX B
COPYRIGHT AND OTHER LEGAL CONSIDERATIONS
by Mary Ann Fergus
Attorney at Law Specializing in Art Law
FergusFirm@earthlink.net
325.676.4818

The statements contained in this writing are not intended as legal advice. You should consult an attorney in your jurisdiction for a legal opinion. Beware that the law varies with each particular fact, circumstance and applicable statute(s).

Painting from Another's Photograph

I receive many questions from Artists about their right to paint from a photograph which was not taken by the Artists themselves. This question involves the doctrine known as "derivative works" in copyright law. The new work is literally derived or taken from the first or original work. This issue is also applicable to other images which may be readily available to an Artist such as images in magazines, postcards, and other such media which we come across in our daily lives. While many Artists are aware that the creator of an image owns the copyright, or right to reproduce their own work, most Artists are unaware about the extent of the right when painting using other's photographs as the basis for the new work. How can the photographs be used without infringing the rights of the photographer? What part of a painting can be taken from another work, and what part may not? Unfortunately, the answer has never been definitively settled in our courts or by the legislature. However, there are a few sound legal principals in this area with which the Artist should be familiar.

U.S. Copyright statues and accompanying case law state clearly that a copyright protection exists in "original works of authorship fixed in any tangible medium of expression . . . which can be perceived, reproduced or otherwise communicated, either directly or with the aid of a machine or device. Works of authorship include. "(5) pictorial, graphic and sculptural works. . ." 17 U.S.C. ¤102 (a). For the visual artist, there is no question that the standard set forth most certainly applies to all original, visual works. That is, the Artist who created the original work [first] owns the copyright. Case law is more illuminating on the subject where you will find the basic theme of the courts to be: the unauthorized reproduction of a copyrighted photograph whether [by another photo] or any other medium is an infringing copy. Epic Metals Corp. v. Condec, Inc. 867 F. Supp. 1009 (M.D. Fla. 1994) (emphasis added.) "Defendants may copy the ideas presented by the Plaintiff's photos, but may not simply make copies of the photograph." Time, Inc. v. Barnard Geis Assoc., 293 F. Supp. 130 (S.D.N.Y. 1968) (emphasis added.) An artist may avoid infringement by intentionally making sufficient changes so that the works at issue undercut "substantial similarity". Warner Bros. v. ABC, 720 F.2d 231, 241 (2d Cir. 1983).

David Renton and Enzo Russo
No Wind
Oil on Canvas
After photographic image courtesy of the
Herreshoff Marine Museum

A 1992 New York case serves as a sound study of the basic principles for artists when copying from photographs while rendering their projects. In Rogers v. Koons, 751 F. Supp. 474 (S.D.N.Y. 1990) aff'd 960 F.2d 301 (2d Cir. 1992) the Appellate Court held that a reproduction of a photograph in a sculpture form constituted an infringement. As applied to the law, the Court found that the facts in this case supported an unauthorized copying on the part of Koons, the Defendant.

Photographer Rogers was hired to photograph his customers, Mr. & Mrs. Scanlon, holding their new German Shepherd puppies in their arms in a black and white format. After the Scanlons purchased their commissioned photograph, Rogers placed the work in his catalog of images for sale as is customary in the trade. Rogers later licensed the work for note cards to Museum Graphics of which 10,000 reproductions were made.

New York sculptor, Jeff Koons, was in the midst of creating a group of 20 sculptures for a gallery exhibit entitled "Banality Show." He was also apparently in the habit of seeking out familiar images from photographs from which to work. In 1987, he came across Roger's note

Appendix B

card in a souvenir shop and determined it contained good composition from which to sculpt. The note card was very similar to other images [of people holding animals] in Koons' file of resource materials. He believed the photograph to be typical, commonplace and familiar and viewed the image as part of the mass culture—"resting in the collective sub-consciousness of people regardless of whether the card had actually ever been seen by such people." Rogers at page 305.

Koons tore off that portion of the note card showing Roger's copyright of "Puppies" and gave it to one of his wood carving workshops in Italy. He then instructed his artisans to copy the photograph in a three-dimensional work. Throughout the fabrication process, Koons oversaw the carving and even gave the workers "production notes" which stated, in no uncertain terms: "work must be just like the photo --- features of the photo must be captured;" later, "Puppies need detail in fur. Details just Like Photo!"; other notes instruct the artisans to keep man in angle of photo. . .Girl's nose is too small. Please make larger as per photo." Rogers at page 305. To paint the polychromed wood "String of Puppies" sculptures, Koons provided artisans with an enlarged photocopy of "Puppies." Painting directions were noted with arrows pointing to the photograph. He writes in his notes: "Paint realistic as per photo, but in blues." and "Man's hair, white with shades of gray as per black and white photo. . . !" (emphasis added.)

When the work was finished, "String of Puppies" was displayed at the Sonnabend Gallery in New York which opened the Banality Show on November 19, 1988. Three of the four copies made were sold to collectors for a total of $367,000; the fourth or artist's copy was kept by Koons. Koons' use of "Puppies" was not authorized by Rogers. Rogers learned of the unauthorized use of his work through his customers, the Scanlons. A friend who was familiar with the work called to tell the Scanlons that a "colorized" version of "Puppies" was on the front page of the activities section of the May 7, 1989 Los Angeles Times. In fact, the newspaper actually depicted Koons' "String of Puppies" in connection with an article about its exhibition at the Los Angeles Museum of Contemporary Art.

Koons maintains he creates his work in an art tradition dating back to the beginning of the Twentieth Century. This tradition defines its efforts as follows: when the artist finishes his work, the meaning of the original object has been extracted and an entirely new meaning is set in its place. An example of this tradition is Andy Warhol's reproduction of multiple images of Campbell Soup cans. Koons' most famous work in this genre is a stainless steel casting of an inflatable rabbit holding a carrot. Rogers at page 304.

Peter S. Robinson
Theresa
Oil on Canvas

    To show an infringement of a copyright, a Plaintiff must show ownership of a copyright; that the Defendant copied the protected material without authorization; and, that the copying was infringing by showing a substantial similarity between the works as relating to the portion of the protected expression. Laureyssens v. Idea Group, 964 F. 2d 131 (2d Cir 1992) see also Feist Publications v. Rural Telephone Service, 111 S. Ct. 1282. The Court first deals with the original authorship/ownership issue. Koons maintains that the portion of Rogers' work allegedly infringed is not [necessarily] an original work of authorship protected under the 1976 Copyright Act. Since that law protects authors' exclusive rights to their works, the cornerstone is that the work must first be original. While a whole work may be copyrighted, this does not mean that every element of it is copyrighted. Copyright protection extends only to those components of the work that are original to the creator. Elements of originality in a photographic image include posing the subjects, lighting, angle, selection of film and camera, evoking the desired expression, and almost any other [creative] variant involved. Rogers at page 307. The quantity of originality that need be shown is modest—only a dash of it will do. 1 M. Nimmer & D., Nimmer, Nimmer on Copyright ¤1.08 (1991). Roger's inventive efforts in posing the group for the photo, taking the picture, and printing "Puppies" suffices to meet the original work of art criteria. Thus, in terms of a unique expression of the subject matter captured in a photograph, Rogers establishes a valid ownership of a copyright in an original work of art.

Appendix B

The next issue considered is whether there is an unauthorized copying of the photograph by sculptor Koons. The Court has no trouble in finding blatant copying by Koons as was supported by the very unusual evidence [for such a case] of the production notes stressing "copy as per photo. . ." Moreover, the importance of copying the very details of the photograph that embodied Rogers' original contribution, such as: the poses, the shading, the expressions, was stressed by Koons throughout the production of the work.

The more complex issue of substantial similarity is then taken up by the Court. Substantial similarity does not require literally identical copying of every detail. Such similarity is determined by the ordinary observer test: the inquiry is "whether an average lay observer would recognize the alleged copy as having been appropriated from the copyrighted work." Ideal Toy Corp. v. Fab-Lu Ltd., 360 F. 2d 1021, 1022 (2d Cir. 1966) Or, stated by another Court, whether "the ordinary observer, unless he set out to detect the disparities, would be disposed to overlook them, and regard their aesthetic appeal as the same." Peter Pan Fabrics v. Martin Weiner Corp., 274 F.2d 487, 489 (2d Cir. 1960).

What is protected [under our copyright laws] is the original or unique way that an author expresses his ideas, concepts, principles or processes. In looking at the two works of art to determine whether they are substantially similar, focus must be on the similarity of expression of an idea or a fact, not on the similarity of the ideas or concepts themselves. Durham Indus. v. Tomy Corp. 630 F.2d 905 (2d Cir. 1980). It is not, therefore, the idea of a couple with eight small puppies seated on a bench which is protected, but rather Roger's expression of this idea — as caught in placement, in the particular light, and in the expressions of the subjects — that gives the photograph its charming and unique character, that is to say, makes it original and copyrightable. Had Koons simply used the idea presented by the photo, there would not have been an infringing copy. But Koons used the identical expression of the idea that Rogers created; the composition, the poses, and the expressions were all incorporated into the sculpture to the extent that, under the ordinary observer test, no reasonable jury could have differed on the issue of substantial similarity. For this reason, the Court held that Koons copied the original photograph in a manner that is substantially similar to the original.

The Court goes on to say that Koons may not defend his act of plagiarism by pointing out how much of the copy he has not pirated. Sheldon v. Metro-Goldwyn Pictures Corp. 81 F. 2d 49, 56 (1936). Where substantial similarity is found, small changes here and there made by the copier are not availing to allow the copy. It is only where the points of dissimilarity exceed those that are similar and those similar are— when compared to the original work—of small import quantitatively or qualitatively that a finding of no infringement is appropriate. Nimmer ¤13.03 [B][1][a]. This is not the case here. Koons' additions, such as flowers in the hair of the couple and the bulbous nose of the puppies, are insufficient in light of the overwhelming similarity to the protected expression of the original work.

The Court then turns to Koons' defense of "fair use" of the image, which is a valid defense in a copyright infringement case. This equitable doctrine permits other people to use copyrighted material without the owner's consent in a reasonable manner for certain purposes. Codified in ¤107 of the 1976 Copyright Act. Section 107 states that an original work copied for purposes such as criticism or comment may not constitute infringement, but instead may be a fair use. The section provides an illustrative—but not exhaustive—list of factors for determining when a use is "fair." These factors include (1) the purpose and character of the use, (2) the nature of the copyrighted work, (3) the amount and substantiality of the work used, and (4) the effect of the use on the market value of the original 17 U.S.C. ¤107. citing Rogers at page 308.

The "purpose and character of the use" asks whether the original was copied in good faith to benefit the public or was it copied primarily for the commercial interests of the infringer. Because it is an equitable doctrine, conduct which intentionally exploits another's work may prevent an artist from using this fair use defense. 3 Nimmer, ¤13.05[A](1). Relevant to this issue is Koons' conduct, especially his action in tearing the copyright mark off of the Roger's note card prior to sending it to the Italian artisans. This action suggests bad faith in Koons' use of Roger's work and militates against a finding [by the Court] of fair use on behalf of Koons. The Supreme Court has previously held that copies made for commercial or profit-making purposes are presumptively unfair. Sony Corp v. Univ. City Studios, Inc. 464 U.S. 417 (1984). The Court also adds that the profit/non-profit distinction is not the only test. But one should also determine whether the user stands to profit from exploitation of the copyrighted material without paying the customary price to the original author. It is obvious in this case that Koons had no intention of paying Rogers for the image in the photograph. citing Rogers at page 209.

The Copyright Act also provides that comment on (parody) or criticism of a copyrighted work may be a valid use under the fair use doctrine. Koons therefore argues his sculpture is a satire or parody of society at large. To support his argument Koons maintains he belongs to a school of American artists who believe that media images and mass production of commodities has caused a deterioration of society. This particular school proposes to incorporate these images into works which comment critically both on the incorporated object as well as the political and economic system which created it. These themes, Koons urges, draw upon the artistic movements of Cubism and Dadaism with particular influence attributed to Marcel Duchamp, who, in 1913, became the first to incorporate manufactured objects (readymades) into a work of art. Duchamp has directly influenced Koons' work and the work of other contemporary American artists. Parody or satire is when one artist, for comic effect or social commentary, closely imitates the style of another artist and in so doing creates a new art work that makes ridiculous the style and expression of the original.

Parody and satire are valued forms of expressions which are encouraged because this sort of criticism fosters the creativity protected by the copyright law. A parody entitles its creator, under the fair use doctrine, to more extensive use of the copied work than is ordinarily allowed under the substantial similarity test. The copied work must be, at least in part, an object of the parody, otherwise there would be no need to conjure up the original work. citing Rogers at page 310. This requirement insists that the audience be aware that, underlying the parody, there is an original and separate expression which is attributable to a different artist. This could come from the fact that the copied work is publicly known or because its existence is in some manner acknowledged by the parodist in connection with the parody. The Court goes to the heart of the problem with Koons' parody defense: "even given that 'String of Puppies' is a satirical critique of our materialistic society, it is difficult to discern any parody of the photograph of "Puppies" itself." The photograph is not the object of a distinct parody from which the audience can draw upon.

The next fair use element asks what is the "nature of the work" that has been copied. The Court considers whether the work is creative, imaginative, or represents an investment of time in anticipation of a financial return. It finds that "Puppies" is indeed creative and imaginative. It is obvious by his actions that Rogers hopes to gain financial return for his efforts with the photograph. Therefore, the Court is unable to support a finding of fair use as to the "nature of the work" aspect of Koons argument. (As an aside, where the original is factual rather than fiction—such as in copying a telephone book compilation—the scope of fair use becomes much broader.)

The Court then turns to the "amount and substantiality" element. It is not fair use when more of the original is copied than is necessary. Even more critical than the quantity is the qualitative degree of copying, that is: what degree of the essence is copied in relation to its whole. In this particular set of facts, the essence of Rogers' photograph was copied nearly in toto, much more than would have been necessary even if the sculpture had been a parody of Roger's work. "In short, it is not really the parody flag that Koons attempts to set sail under, but rather the flag of piracy." citing Rogers at page 309.

As for effect of the use on the market value of the original, the Court refers to its previous finding that Koons intended his copy of Rogers' work be created solely for commercial gain. An owner of a copyright need only show that the unauthorized use of a copy could potentially become so widespread so as to prejudice the potential market for the original work. The reason for this rule relates to a central concern of copyright law: that unfair copying undercuts demand for the original work and, as an inevitable consequence, chills creation of such works.

The Rogers v. Koons opinion represents the prevailing view on derivative works. Rogers was successful in showing: 1) ownership of a valid copyright in an original work; 2) unauthorized copying by Koons; and 3) that the copying was substantially similar and therefore an infringement on Roger's photographic work. The fair use defense was not available to Koons on any one of the four factors enumerated. The most likely factor which he could have prevailed upon would have been the parody or satire element. However, as his copying was so blatant and ill-intentioned, the Court was not able to find any indices of parody in his work.

As an artist, it is important to be aware of the elements of a valid copyright ownership. Your work is valuable and you should always strive to protect its value in any situation. Additionally, you should be thinking about what resources can be utilized, without an infringement, from other creative works, should the need arise. You might ask yourself when utilizing another's work for resource material: would you be in violation of any of the elements of a copyright infringement as stated above? Do you need to seek appropriate authorization from the creator of the work? Does the situation warrant calling in a legal expert?

Stay "tuned in" to where you stand when using resource material that you did not create yourself. It is important to know these distinctions and draw upon them as necessary in rendering your projects. Do not put yourself in a position where you must guess which is appropriate for use in your work, and which is not. Consult an expert when in doubt, and always enter into a written agreement with your clients/agents setting forth the details of your commission works.

Sale and Purchase of Work

All sales, whether commissioned work or otherwise, should have a written agreement between the parties. If you have the luxury of selling your work prior to its execution (i.e. a commissioned work) be careful to set out all-important foundations of the sale. Protect your copyright. And remember that you own the copyright in the work you created beyond your death, not the purchaser of the work.

If you sell your work through a gallery or agent, you should also have a written contract to protect your interests.

Record of Art Work

It is important to keep a photo and written file reference for each work sold as well as significant and favorite other works (or series of work) you have created but not sold. You may find it convenient to use a three ring binder for this purpose. In addition to preserving your authorship and Copyright, it enhances the value of a work to track the history with your notes. It is worth the effort and cost to seek assistance with record keeping. Create a file on each major subject and/or work with notes and images. Organize your files on a regular basis. Archive your records in a safe location. Your patrons will seek out this information as your career unfolds. Do not allow a painting be placed without a record of the image.

Appendix B

Registration of Art Work

You should always register your work in the United Sates with the U.S. Copyright Office. Why register a work? The registration concept now works in favor of a copyright owner to protect the artwork against unlawful infringement. Historically, the law favored those benefits derived by the public from the labors of the artist. This is no longer the case. Formal registration automatically gives expanded rights to the owner of a copyright in the United States. Different laws apply to different countries.

Please note that this information is for educational purposes and is intended only as a guide for you to learn about the registration process. To register your work, you must walk through a few steps. First, review the instructions at the Patent Office web site. The copyright office is a subdivision of the Patent Office. Once your artwork is complete, take two photo images of your artistic rendering (the painting) and complete the application Form VA and Form CON (if needed). You may download the forms and print them out. Include the registration fee (at this writing the fee is $45). The photo images of your work are not returnable. The process involves filling out the form(s) attaching the photo images and including the filing fee in an envelope. Mail the registration items to: Library of Congress, 101 Independence Ave., S.E., Washington, D.C. 20559-6000. Your registration is effective the day that it is received by the Library of Congress in acceptable form. You will receive a Certificate of Registration in about four months. Keep the registration certificate along with your record of the work.

Donation of Work

Artists are frequently asked to donate work for auction or sale to support philanthropy. It is tempting to submit work for obvious marketing reasons. It is also common for artists to have strong feelings about a particular cause. Artists are, after all, deeply passionate about this world. If possible, keep donations of work to a minimum, especially commissioned work in a low profile charitable setting. Strive to vary your donations from one charitable organization to another. Investigate your potential purchasers prior to agreeing to donate work. Set a reasonable minimum for the bidding process to prevent devaluation of your work. Consider donation of reproductions of your work as appropriate. Federal tax law does not favor deduction of artist donation. State tax laws vary. Consult a tax expert for all questions regarding this aspect.

Copyright Basics

What can be copyrighted? The law sets forth the principle that copyright protects the expression of an idea, but not the idea itself. For example, you can paint the sky in a special way, but you cannot own the idea of the sky. Once an artist reveals his work to the public, he injects the idea into the public domain and must be content to seek control over the form in which his idea has been expressed. To create new work, artists must have access to a well-endowed public domain where creative concepts are freely available to an artist who would embellish the concepts with his own expression.

The primary elements [of owning the copyright] for a visual artwork require that 1: the work have originality and 2: the work be "fixed in a medium." For painters, the artwork is fixed in a medium when a paint product is applied to the canvas or the support.

The owner of the right to copy can reproduce that work in any way available. The owner can further use the work (straight out copying) as a basis for a new work or a derivative work. The owner can, for example, make reproductions of the work, digitize and disseminate the work (distribute), display the work in public (think of computer screens in public spaces).

You will need to ask permission and/or pay a fee to use another's material that is copyright protected. There are three known limited exceptions for using another's work: Fair Use, Library's Special Rights, and Educational displays. Exemptions to copyright have been applied conservatively in some jurisdictions of the U.S., and more liberally in others. Remember also, even if the work is not covered by copyright law, it may be protected by other laws (e.g. right of privacy, foreign laws, rights of publicity and the like). If you have any question about your particular set of facts, you should consult an attorney for advice.

Enzo Russo and David Renton
Portrait of Doug Birdsall
Oil on Canvas

Former U.S. Copyright law afforded protection of copyright by the owner giving an actual copyright notice. The fixing of a copyright notice no longer carries the importance that was critical before 1978. As of the date of this writing, U.S. Copyright protection attaches to a work the minute it is created and fixed in a medium. The corollary regarding the artist's right to copy his own work, also known as a copyright, is also immediately fixed in the expression of the work (i.e. the canvas holding the paint.)

Another important issue is whether a creation is a "Work for Hire." When an employee creates artwork for an employer, all of the rights created within the employment relation attach to the employer. If you are an illustrator for a large entertainment company for example, and your time at work is spent creating characters for the employer, then the employer owns the copyright to the work. Free lance artists are presumed to retain copyright in their work. An art purchaser may insist that a work "be for hire" which becomes important if the work is part of a large art effort (e.g. an art rendering at a public space). If the agreement is in writing and contains language indicating a work for hire situation, then the copyright will be owned by the one who commissioned the work.

Appendix B

Any work published on or before December 31, 1922 is now in the public domain. Works that have been published between January 1, 1923 and December 31, 1978, are protected for 95 years from date of publication, but with an appropriate (full and proper) notice. Some works may not have protection under these laws.

If the work was published between 1923 and December 31, 1963, during the non-renewal period, the copyright owner may not have renewed the work. If there was no renewal, the original term of protection (28 years) has expired and the work is in the public domain.

After the year 1978, *death of the creator* is the measurement of the term to a work that is protected. It is no longer linked to the work's date of publication. The term runs for 70 years from the date the artist dies (this is referred to as life of the creator plus 70 years). Publication of a work is no longer relevant after 1978. Works are protected whether or not they are published, as stated earlier: the work is protected once it has been fixed on the canvas.

How does infringement of a copyright occur, and how does the owner enforce his right? A copyright infringer is someone who violates any of the exclusive rights of the copyright owner under the law. Just as there are nuances in color and shading, there are nuances in knowing what is copying another's work. Always ask yourself "is this work protected?" If you suspect a work may be copyright protected, take steps to procure permission. See a copyright attorney if you want to review the possibility that you have infringed or someone has infringed your creative property (your artwork).

A work may be in the "public domain." Public domain has been described as the body of knowledge and inventions, creative art, writing, music, in relation to which no person or other legal entity can establish or maintain a proprietary interest within a particular legal jurisdiction. In general, anyone may use or exploit, whether for commercial or non-commercial purposes, a work that is in the public domain.

This footnote is a brief and limited introduction to the copyright laws of the United States. As always, seek the advice of a legal expert in the field of copyright for your specific facts and issues. Manage your intellectual property and stay informed of your rights. As the creator of artwork, you are the parent launching your artistic child into the world of fixed medium. You cannot always be on hand to protect your creation.

Remember you should not substitute the information of this writing for that of a copyright lawyer. This article is not definitive, and contains limited information about the subject. It is not intended to be a substitute for legal counsel. Always seek an expert in the jurisdiction you seek to protect your right.

Made in the USA
Lexington, KY
17 August 2010